THE HISTORY OF TRALEE

Its Charter and Governance

Gerald O'Carroll

First published in 2009

Copyright © Gerald O'Carroll

ISBN 978-0-9547902-2-6

Printed by Kingdom Printers, Matt Talbot Road, Tralee

In memoriam Fr Ragheed Ganni,
Iraq 2007

CONTENTS

CONTENTS

LIST OF ILLUSTRATIONS

LIST OF ABBREVIATIONS

Cal. S. P.: *Calendar of State Papers*

D. J.: *Faulkner's Dublin Journal*

F. J.: *The Freeman's Journal*

H. C. Jn. (Ir.): *Irish House of Commons Journal*

H. C.: *Hibernian Chronicle*

H. M. C.: *Historic Mss. Commission, Ormond*

I. T.: *Irish Times*

J. C. H. A. S.: *Journal of the Cork Historical and Archaeological Society*

J. H. A. A. I.: *Journal of the Historical and Arch. Association of Ireland*

J. K. A. H. S.: *Journal of the Kerry Arch. and Hist. Society.*

J. R. S. A. I.: *Journal of the Royal Society of Antiquaries Ireland*

K. E. P.: *Kerry Evening Post*

L. C.: *Limerick Chronicle*

M. N.: *Munster News and Provincial Advertiser*

N. A. I.: *National Archives of Ireland*

N. L. I.: *National Library of Ireland*

FOREWORD

This fascinating book illuminates the complicated relationships, alliances and divisions in this far corner of Ireland, which also exemplify, in part, the history of the whole country. Who/what is an Irishman? My father, Sir Henry Denny, was a genealogist and historian, a founder of the County Kerry Society and lifelong student of Irish and English families and the history of these islands. He would have been delighted with the immense research which has resulted in this work. Our family, closely involved with Tralee from the 16th to the 20th centuries, perpaps exemplifies the extraordinary complications and conflicts of loyalties in Ireland. They considered themselves, at times or all at once, Irish, English, Anglo Irish, United Irish or Absentees, and all these before religion and politics were stirred into the pot. They also intermarried with families from all layers of Irish history – Gaelic, Norman and Elizabethan English.

God preserve the peace now in Ireland and best wishes for this important book.

Sir Anthony Denny

PREFACE

Much of this book is the work of research recovery. A number of gifted historians of Kerry in the nineteenth and early twentieth centuries, including Rev. Archdeacon Rowan (d. 1861), Mary Agnes Hickson (d. 1899) and the Rev. Sir Henry Lyttelton Lyster Denny (d.1953), did the important spade work, to which I added work on some of the documentary sources, such as the Journals of the old Irish House of Commons, and other published primary sources. The earls of Desmond, who preceded the Dennys and ruled Tralee for about three hundred years, have been well covered in the old academic journals, and there is some important recent research. Tralee is central to the Desmond story, and Holy Cross, the Dominican house they founded in the town, became their burial place. Important Denny material was donated to the Victoria and Albert Museum by Sir Edward Denny, 4th Baronet (1796-1889) and by Rev. Sir H. L. L. Denny, 7th Bart. already mentioned. I am grateful to Sir Anthony Denny for assistance with this book and for the use of portrait images of his ancestors. The Knight of Glin loaned me the Blennerhassetts Pedigree, which corroborated the official genealogies as well as the publications of Russell McMorran on the subject. Sean Kelly of Newcastle West gave me a copy of G.O. Sayles's article on Maurice, first Earl of Desmond. The publications of the Kerry Archaeological and Historical Society over the last forty years have covered all the important questions in Kerry history; I have visited the Kerry County Library and used these extensively. Niall O'Brien of Co. Waterford shared his knowledge of the Desmond property in the Decies, Youghal and Inchiquin. Jim Reidy showed me the homes of the gentry around Castleisland. For portrait images and scenes I am grateful to Ann Elter, Paddy Waldron, Pat Melville-Baker, Donald Cameron, Lar Dunne, Maurice O'Keeffe, John O'Flaherty and Pat FitzGerald, and of course Anthony Denny. George Rice of Tralee and Des Long of Limerick assisted with advice on Kerry during the War of Independence and the Civil War. To the Granary (Limerick City) Library and Mike Maguire I am once again deeply indebted, as I am to the staff at the new County Library (Dooradoyle) for showing me how to use the digital search engine in the *Irish Times*. The Granary has all the genealogical books, including Burke's and *The Complete Peerage*. Mike Brosnan, Sean Moraghan, Liam Clifford and Michael Rice read proofs and made valuable suggestions. I am grateful to Eamon Dillon of Listowel for the loan of Foley's *History of Kerry and Corkaguiney* and *O'Sullivan's Romantic Hidden Kerry*, both of which are long out of print; also to Matthew Potter who offered much advice on the politics of the nineteenth century, and to Shane Lehane who wrote a fine thesis on the Famine.

INTRODUCTION

The Anglo-Normans, founders of Tralee, arrived at Wexford in the South East of Ireland in 1169. They had predecessors in the pagan Vikings of the ninth century who attacked the monasteries and left their mark in certain place names near the Shannon estuary. The Anglo-Normans, rather than the Viking, effected the greater transformation of Gaelic civilization, by means of new monastic foundations, novel agricultural practices and civil institutions including the king's courts and town charters. This positive contribution is worth bearing in mind when we come to consider the sharp religious differences that mark the reconquest of Kerry in the sixteenth century at the time of Queen Elizabeth and again under the generals of Oliver Cromwell in the following century.

St Brendan, patron saint of Kerry, was born at Ardfert. The first bishop of the diocese (the diocese of Ardfert) was Erc. Christianity remained characteristically insular, the extreme expression of which was the settlement of the Skellig rock by monks whose patron was St Michael. When Irish monks spearheaded the re-evangelisation of Europe in the time of Charlemagne (crowned Holy Roman Emperor in 800), the evidence suggests that regions other than Kerry played a greater part. Later, the Anglo-Normans caused a proliferation of monastic foundations, but the Cistercians had preceded the Anglo-Norman arrival in Ireland by about a generation. Their first foundation was Mellifont, in Co. Louth. Its first abbot was Christian O' Conarchy who became bishop of Lismore and ended his days at Abbeydorney, the Cistercian foundation just north of Tralee. He was the Pope's legate when King Henry II came over from England to exert some measure of control over that first wave of invaders. O'Conarchy was at the council at Cashel which recognised Henry's claim to rule Ireland under the bull *Laudabiliter* given to Henry by the Pope.

It was often the native Gaelic clans who, during the twelfth and succeeding centuries, violated the centres of civilization including the churches and monasteries. The hostile geography of the South of Kerry, controlled by clans like the MacCarthys, confined the Anglo-Normans to the more hospitable region North of the rivers Laune and Maine, which became the historic *County* of Kerry. However, with isolation from the centre of power, and through intermarriage with the Irish, the Anglo-Irish marcher lords became *more Irish than the Irish themselves*. The Elizabethans, like the Anglo-Normans, maintained considerable dealings with the native Irish, so when the Elizabethan Valentine Brown settled at Molahiffe, a Gaelic wife was found for his heir. The pattern was set, and even after the bitter War of Three Kings (1688-91) when the Dutchman William supplanted the legitimate James, there existed the kind of mutual understanding between the races which was founded on intermarriage and shared religious allegiance. Nevertheless, Tralee became a citadel of conquest and privilege, Denny and Blennerhassett presiding over an exclusive urban corporation. Divisions emerged quickly among the leading settlers when the Dennys showed a greater allegiance to the historic monarchy than did the less armigerous Blennerhassetts; and though both were connected to powerful families outside of Kerry, the rivalry renewed when the leading Dennys escaped attainder in the Jacobite Parliament of 1689. Tralee Castle, seat of the Desmond earls and later the Dennys, provided the thematic unity for the first section of this book, as did the grant of the town Charter in 1613 for the section to follow; then comes a century of rivalry among the settlers from, say, 1692, which has escaped critical examination until now, finally the overthrow of the oligarchy in the second quarter of the nineteenth century by the dynasty of Daniel O'Connell, *the Liberator*, prefiguring the age of popular democracy and the independent Irish state.

ONE
PALATINATE

1. THE ANGLO-NORMAN ADVANCE INTO NORTH KERRY

The founders of Tralee came originally from Normandy, in the north of France, invading Ireland from Wales where they had settled after the Norman invasion of England in 1066. So it would be more accurate to call them Cambro-Normans. King Henry II, who sponsored the invasion of Ireland, retained very strong links with France both as son of Geoffrey of Anjou and husband of Eleanor of Aquitaine: "Your victories (wrote Giraldus Cambrensis, chronicler of the Irish invasion) vie with the whole round of the world. Our western Alexander, you have stretched your arm from the Pyrenean mountains even to these far western bounds of the northern ocean."

Some of the leading Kerry conquistadors descended from a Welsh princess by the name of Nesta. Her husband was Gerald of Windsor. They were the parents of Maurice FitzGerald who came to Ireland with Henry; Maurice's son would become one of the leaders of the Cambro-Norman advance into North Kerry and ancestor of the southern Geraldines. Nesta was also the sometime mistress of King Henry I, by whom she bore Meiler FitzHenry, one of the first grantees of land in the North of Kerry.

After the Kingdom of Cork was divided between Cogan and FitzStephen, a daughter of Cogan married Simon le Poher, who enfeoffed William de Burgh with Altry, the northernmost division of Kerry, and Acumys, the division in which Tralee stands.[1] (Each territorial division was called a *triúcha céad*, which is found in the name of the barony of which Tralee became the capital: Trughan*acmy*.) The de Burgh grants also included the baronies of modern West Limerick which lie closest to Kerry, including Shanid, and it was from this direction that Kerry was invaded.

The principal Anglo-Norman lords of Kerry were of the Geraldine family, descendants of Maurice FitzGerald already mentioned. His son, Tomás Mór (+1213), was the first of them. Tomás was part of de Burgh's invasion of Kerry, and when, in 1200, King John superseded de Burgh's grant with a grant to Meiler FitzHenry (Tomás Mór's cousin), Tomás was part of Meiler's advance into Kerry; and then, before Meiler resigned all his worldly possessions and entered a monastery, Tomás Mór was part of Meiler's conquest of Trughanacmy. The dates were perhaps 1205-7.[2]

Geoffrey de Marisco founded a preceptory of the Knights Hospitaller at Any (modern Knockainy, Co. Limerick), as well as the Augustinian priory at Killagh, near Milltown. The Knights Hospitaller are said to have established a house in Tralee from Any, on the site of the present church of St John's in Ashe Street. It was called Teampall an tSoluis, the *Light* in question a reminder of the welcome prepared for the traveller.

De Clahull, another Anglo-Norman family, was dominant in the division of Offerba, which contained the ring of territory around Tralee Bay which would in modern times become the Denny estate. Tralee may have been eclipsed in this early period by castles like Tawlaght, the principal castle of Offerba, and the port of Tralee by the more important sea access of Barrow Harbour. Mary Hickson believed that "All things considered, Fenit, as the port of Ardfert, had the advantage of Tralee from 1230 to 1329 when the Earldom of Desmond was created". She cited as evidence the preponderance of another Anglo-Norman family, FitzMaurice of Ardfert and Lixnaw, that Ardfert was the seat of the diocesan Bishop, and that "three strong castles (Barrow, Fenit and Tallaght), built on the verge of the water, kept close watch over the old port and river of Fenit before 1587". It was through Barrow (Fenit) Harbour that the wine importers of Dingle dispersed the casks of wine destined for their greatest market: the many FitMaurice's possessions in Clanmaurice.[3]

2. JOHN OF SHANID, FOUNDER OF TRALEE

The son of Tomás Mór was John of Shanid, *aka* John of Callan from the place where he met his death.[4] John's gaze was turned east because his FitzAnthony wife brought him the territory of Decies in modern Waterford (which would be confirmed to their descendants). But he found time to consolidate his grip on West Limerick. And he founded the town of Tralee.

Fragments of the old Abbey in the Priory garden

The essential infrastructure for a Norman town was put in place: a castle, a principal street – to be known as Burgess St – and a market place adorned with a market cross where people would go to hear proclamations and news reports. In 1243, he established the Dominican Abbey under the invocation of the Holy Cross. The Abbey expanded in an impressive complex of buildings south of the present Square, owning also property beyond the limits of the town, with the result that Holy Cross became perhaps the most extensive Dominican property in Ireland. The founder and his son would be buried there after the great defeat at Callan, and later it would become the sepulchre of their descendants, the Geraldine earls. The Desmond Survey (1584) tells us that vessels of up to five tons could come right up to the walls of the Abbey. Quays were built that survived to the middle of the nineteenth century, long enough to be seen by the first residents of Day Place, by which time the channel had become silted up and Blennerville was starting to come into its own as the port of Tralee. The fact that only fragments of Holy Cross survive is testimony to the scale of destruction wrought by the suppression of the Geraldine earldom in the reign of Queen Elizabeth I (1558-1603).[5]

The great Castle of Tralee stood on the site of the present Denny Street. It was always considered a gloomy pile: Archdeacon Rowan (+1861) described it as "a huge pile of blank walls without even a window to break its dead front as it extended across the site of Denny Street".[6] An attempt was made by the Dennys about 1804 to make it more habitable: "It was a building partly ancient and partly modern, turning its back on the Main Street or Mall, and extending its front looking southwards for nearly 300 feet over what used to be called the 'Bowling Green'."[7] It was pulled down in 1826 to make way for the development of Denny Street.

The Anglo-Normans founded incorporated boroughs at Tralee, Ardfert, Dingle, Rattoo and Aghadoe, though none of their charters survive. Ardfert already existed as an ecclesiastical centre, providing a road infrastructure in the form of converging routes, but Tralee and Dingle were new towns, both situated on the sea at points likely to develop well as ports, Tralee perhaps yielding to the additional attraction of location near the old church at Rattass.[8]

South of the rivers Maine and Laune, the region that would contain the County of Desmond lacked the civic and urban settlement which the Anglo-Normans brought to the North, where Tralee is situated; however, the MacCarthys of Killarney and the South continued to pay tribute to the earls of Desmond right up to the sixteenth century, and the Battle of Callan (near Kilgarvan) in 1261, which cost the life of John, founder of Tralee, and his heir, Maurice, was not the straight fight between Anglo-Norman and the native MacCarthys as is conventionally believed.[9]

3. WHEN AN APE STOLE THE GERALDINE HEIR AND TOOK HIM TO THE TOP OF THE ABBEY

Maurice's infant heir is the subject of the following episode, which takes place when the news of Callan reaches Tralee.

"This Thomas, being in his swaddling cloaths accidently left alone in his cradle, was by an Ape carried up to the battlements of the monastery of Traly, where the little beast, to the admiration of the many spectators, dandled him to and froe, whilst everyone ran with theire beds and caddows (tartans), thinking to catch the child when it should fall from the Ape. But Divine providence prevented that danger; for the Ape miraculously bore away the infant, and left him in the cradle as he found him, by which accident this Thomas was ever after nicknamed from The Ape."[10]

Floor tile, with the Desmond Boar, from Tralee Castle.

Another tradition places the child at the top of the Castle, not the Abbey: his nurse, in a state of upset after hearing the dismal tidings from Callan, has left her charge alone in his cradle, from which the ape removes him and takes him aloft. There the ape removes the infant's swaddling clothes, licks him all over, dresses him and returns him safely to his cradle. Then, for her neglect, the ape delivers the nurse a blow to the face.[11] The folk memory of Thomas *An Appagh* (+1298) is still green in the district of Newcastle West which competed with Tralee as a centre of Geraldine power. Thomas Johnson Westropp, eminent antiquarian and native to that district, remembered hearing a ballad with the line, "the berry-brown *nuppagh*, the *nuppagh* of merry Tralee".[12] The Ape story is to be found also in the tradition of the Leinster Geraldines, with the difference that the Ape survives in the family crest, while the Munster Geraldines adopted the Boar.

The minority of Thomas *An Appagh* encouraged the kind of turmoil predictable at such times, but when Thomas reached his majority he led an impressive series of campaigns to restore the status quo, and such was his resulting prestige that he was appointed king's justiciar in Ireland. The King, Edward I (1272-1307) expanded royal power into Scotland and Wales, and Thomas's wife, Margaret de Burgh, is referred to in the State Papers as "the King's Cousin", from which we may infer that Thomas was a leading vassal of the King in the marches of the Irish South West. Thomas is believed to be the founder of the Novo Castro (today's Newcastle West); in 1286 Parliament gave a murage grant for the construction of a town wall around Tralee (apparently never built) "in aid of inclosing his vills of Traylli, Moyal (Mallow), and Ard (Ardfert?), for the security and safe keeping of those vills and the neighbouring parts".[13] Then, on 6 February 1292, King Edward confirmed to Thomas his grandfather's acquisition of Decies, together with the custody of the castle of Dungarvan".[14]

The inquisition taken shortly after Thomas An Appagh's death in 1298 reveals the extent of his interests in West Limerick, apart from Kerry: he is seized of the manors of Newcastle West, of Shanid, and of Mallow, as well as the manor of Killorglin, "and the manor de Insula (Castleisland)" in the same county.[15] He died at New Castle and was brought to Tralee to lie beside his father and grandfather, who had lost their lives at Callan.

4. ENGLAND EMBROILED WITH FRANCE: THE GERALDINES AS DEGENERATE IRISH

What old historians referred to as the *degeneration* of the Anglo-Norman colony, its becoming "more Irish than the Irish themselves", commenced in the fourteenth century. Changed circumstances in England and internationally meant that Thomas *an Appagh's* heir, Maurice, first Earl of Desmond, had little incentive to replicate his father's loyalism.[16] When Maurice succeeded his father in 1314 the new King, Edward II (1307-1327), was already surrounded by those male companions who insulated him from his people and interfered with the good governance of the realm. A Scots insurrection under Robert Bruce culminated in the defeat of the English at Bannockburn, followed by the arrival of Bruce's brother at Larne in the North-East of Ireland and the opening of an Irish front. Bruce pressed as far south as Limerick. About the same time, the Gaelic overthrow of the Anglo-Norman de Clare at the battle of Dysert O'Dea in 1318 revived an old claim for Maurice to some of the de Clare territory, a claim which Maurice attempted to make good over the next number of years. The clans of Killarney and south sought to capitalise on the instability, though when the leading MacCarthy was murdered on the bench at the Assizes in Tralee in 1325 it was not with Maurice's connivance. Despite numerous complaints about his cruelty, and perhaps in an effort to placate him, Maurice was made Earl of Desmond in 1329, two years after the accession of the great king Edward III (1327-1377).

The grant of the earldom greatly enhanced the status of Tralee. Castleisland may have been the Geraldine's favourite seat, though the Geraldine chief tended to move about with his retinue from castle to castle as the need and the season required, but this changed with the grant of the earldom. Kerry now became a Palatinate where the Earl exercised semi-royal powers, Tralee as his capital, the seat of his Palatine court. We learn from the Desmond Survey that Tralee hosted a "great session for the government", and that the Earl's tenants were obliged to attend, paying for the lodgings and sustenance of the Earl and his retinue, their wives doing the work of cooking.[17] As the new king took his country to war with France in 1337, beginning the Hundred Years War, Maurice threatened his local rivals, the Anglo-Norman Fitzmaurice, of Lixnaw, also directing his *Desmond's rout* at the powers in neighbouring Cork. In 1339 at Currans he captured the leader of the FitzMaurices and had him thrown into prison and starved to death. To check the Earl, the Justiciar, Ufford, invaded Munster and captured Castleisland. Maurice made peace, and he may have joined the war in Europe about the time the king's son, the Black Prince, won the great victory of Crécy (1346). He was back to witness the outbreak of the Black Death (1348), and when he died in 1356 he was brought for burial to Tralee and Holy Cross.

Effigy of Edward II at Gloucester Cathedral

There are two short earldoms, then the fourth Earl, Gerald, the *Poet* Earl, who reigns for about thirty years. His contemporary is King Richard II (1377-1399), successor to his grandfather, King Edward III. The *Poet,* or *Wizard,* Earl is a legendary figure, like *An Appagh*: when he died he was doomed to ride across the waters of Lough Gur in Limerick every seven years until his horse's silver shoes wore down on the ripples of the lake. For Tralee historian Fr Dominic O'Daly, he was "a man remarkable for prudence and military renown". But the degree of attention Gerald devoted to Tralee is difficult to know. His wife was a Butler, from the family of the earls of Ormond, which probably distracted his attention to his inheritance in the East, but the international war contributed to leaving him to his own devices. England was tempted into a renewal of the war with France in the 1380s when Burgundy, under Duke Philip *the Bold* (le Hardi +1404), emerged as a rival to France, Philip having greatly expanded his territory through his marriage to Margaret of Flanders, the territory of modern Belgium. England, in pursuit of her own *wool* policy, saw Flanders, the great market for her wool exports, as an ally; in the 1380s John of Gaunt, brother of the Black Prince and uncle of King Richard, opened a separate front against France in Portugal where his daughter had married Portugal's king. Meanwhile there was such a degree of turbulence in Ireland that King Richard landed at Waterford in 1394 with a large army and began making agreements with the clans.

5. Zenith of Desmond Power: the Usurper Seventh Earl, James, burial in Tralee

Desmond power reaches its zenith in the fifteenth century. Thomas, grandson of the Poet Earl, succeeded as sixth Earl while still a minor and a ward of his cousins the Butlers. He was in power when the English resumed their winning ways with the victory of Henry V at Agincourt (1415). But he was of a romantic temperament, perhaps a throwback to the age of the troubadours of the previous century. While hunting one night in the environs of Portrinard Castle (near Abbeyfeale), nightfall or the weather compelled him to take shelter at the house of one MacCormack. He became infatuated with MacCormack's daughter, Catherine, and when love successfully circumvented society's prohibitions, including the Statutes of Kilkenny drawn up to keep the races apart, they married. The upshot was that his uncle James "thrice expelled him from his lands and obliged him in the presence of (Butler) the Earl of Ormond and others to make a formal surrender of the earldom". The deposed Earl exiled himself to France, dying in 1420 at Rouen, where it is said that Henry V attended his funeral.[18]

James, the *Usurper* seventh Earl of Desmond (1416-1462) was a contemporary of the weak and long-reigned Henry VI who brought England into the civil wars known as the Wars of the Roses. When Earl James came to power through the overthrow of his nephew, England's weakness was not immediately apparent: the victory of Agincourt had put her decisively ahead in her struggle with France, and the new Duke of Burgundy, John the Fearless (*Sans Peur*), was proving a ruthlessly effective ally. It was not a scenario likely to encourage the new Earl to dabble in continental affairs. Instead, Earl James bided his time and ingratiated himself with the Irish. He assumed Gaelic ways: having been fostered among the O'Briens of Thomond, and succeeded to the earldom by the Irish custom of *tanistry* (merit rather than primogeniture), he surrounded himself with those *filí* (poets) so feared by the English for their influence on Gaelic chiefs. From the full accession of Henry VI in 1422 the House of Lancaster began to totter to its knees. The young king's descent from the usurper Henry IV, a son of John of Gaunt, made him vulnerable to overthrow by the senior line with a better claim; he came under pressure to make good his claim to France; and it was commonly believed that he was dominated by his queen, Margaret of Anjou.

"The Meeting on the Turret Stairs", Frederick William Burton

Earl James signed a treaty with the FitzMaurices at Castleisland in 1422 which appears to have sealed the subjugation of that family to the Earls.[19] With Ireland threatening to slip from the king's grasp, the Earl was appointed Governor of Limerick Castle in 1423, and he acquired the title deeds to the former Cogan territory west of Cork Harbour. He re-edified, or perhaps founded, the Franciscan house at Askeaton, built the Halla Mór and the keep nearby, and the Desmond Hall at Newcastle West.[20]

The Friary, Askeaton, by Beranger

Yet it is possible to trace the destruction of the Desmond earls to the era of James and to a fatal fascination – one shared by many other Irish magnates – with the cause of the White Rose of York and that house's efforts to overthrow King Henry VI. Richard, Duke of York arrived at Howth in 1449 as Irish Viceroy. In October Earl James and the fourth Earl of Ormond acted as sponsors at the baptism of York's son George, the future Duke of Clarence. The baptism took place in Dublin Castle.[21] Though Henry VI and Margaret were victorious in 1460 at Wakefield, and Richard Duke of York killed in the battle, York's son, Edward, won the throne in early 1461 at the battle of Towton and prepared to reign as Edward IV. It must have appeared that the Irish, including the Earl of Desmond, had backed the right side in the English conflict.

Earl James died the following year. There is conflicting evidence about his final resting place. Westropp has him buried in the Friary in Youghal, but O'Cleary gives Tralee. The year 1462 seems generally agreed.[22] The *Book of Pedigrees* has the following: "In Caislean Nua Ó Conaill (Newcastle West) he died after the ending of his age, and he was buried in Tralee, 1462."

6. JUDICIAL MURDER OF THOMAS, EIGHTH EARL OF DESMOND: THE BEGINNING OF DECLINE

"A great deed was done in Drogheda this year; to wit, the Earl of Desmond ... was beheaded. And the learned relate that there was not ever in Ireland a foreign youth that was better then he. And he was killed in treachery by a Saxon Earl ..."

(The *Annals of Ulster*)

Thomas, eighth Earl, paid with his life for his father's greatness, but he was the victim also of some intense rivalry at the heart of Irish government and at the King's court. Though he was appointed Lord Deputy of Ireland by the King, he was executed at Drogheda in 1468, then brought to Tralee for burial.

Historians have struggled to explain the judicial murder of Thomas, and the subject has given rise to many learned articles. One tradition is that he had been indiscreet in something he said in the hearing of King Edward's IV's Queen, Elizabeth Woodville. King Edward, who is said to have had a great personal liking for Earl Thomas, asked him one day if there was any aspect of his kingship that he should change. Thomas is said to have advised him to reconsider his marriage to Elizabeth, the daughter of Woodville, a low-ranking private gentleman. The King confided this to the Queen, who began to think of schemes to destroy Thomas. (The choice of Elizabeth Woodville had dashed the hopes of King Edward's principal adviser, the Earl of Warwick, who had aspirations for a lady from his own family and who now departed for France to launch a Lancastrian invasion.) Another suggested reason for the destruction of Thomas is that he collected *coign and livery*, proscribed by the Crown, just as any Gaelic chief did. Earl Thomas's private interests were extensive. He had a Barry wife and his extensive family and official business drew his attention to the territory around Youghal. Earl Thomas's defenders (they include the historian Thomas Russell, 1638) countered by pointing to Thomas's participation in the English civil war in some of the great battles against the Lancastrians.

The *Annals of the Four Masters* tell us that Thomas was buried at Tralee. Then his followers attacked the Pale around Dublin in wave after wave, but their anger concealed the growing divisions which began to surface among them. They also pondered how to enlist the support of foreign powers to drive the English out of Ireland, and the port of Dingle would be a useful point of embarkation for their ambassadors to go and seek such support. The new Earl, Thomas's son James, was in power for a brief Lancaster interregnum and for the recovery of the throne by King Edward in 1471, and he remained Earl through the reign of the deeply unpopular King Richard III (1483-85). Richard sent presents to James together with reassurances of his personal remorse at the execution of his father, but it was King Richard's successor, the Lancastrian Tudor, Henry VII, who would bear the brunt of the Desmond fury at Earl Thomas's execution.

7. THE NINTH EARL, JAMES; DINGLE, AND AN ALLY IN BURGUNDY

During the later Middle Ages the port of Dingle was the principal point of embarkation for pilgrims to Santiago de Compostella in Galicia, Spain. In addition, traders from Dingle might attend the great fairs of Flanders and return safely without being intercepted by the English navy, and they might bring with them envoys from the earls of Desmond to the political representatives of England's enemies. Dingle was an important source of the Earls' wealth in import and export duties. The Desmond Survey noted the "customs and subsidies" that accrued to the earls on imported and exported goods at the ports of "Dingle, Bantry, Smerwick, Ardecanny, and other places".

Henry Tudor came to the throne when he defeated Richard III at Bosworth in 1485, and Henry's marriage to Elizabeth of York united the two conflicting sides in the Wars of the Roses. Eventhough England's civil war was at an end, modern research has shown how much the earls of Desmond, despite the threat posed by a newly united England under Henry, maintained their links with Burgundy. We learn that Earl James and his heir, Maurice, "cultivated political and diplomatic contacts with the duchy of Burgundy and the kingdom of France through their trading links with Bruges and Bordeaux".[23] What tempted them was the fact that the Countess of Burgundy, wife of Duke Charles the Bold, was the sister of the deposed Edward IV, and yet it seems utterly illogical to us today that they would scheme against the new monarchy with the dynasty that had murdered their ancestor at Drogheda. To make matters worse, their rivals in East Munster, the Butlers, earls of Ormond, supported the Tudors. Is their dabbling in foreign diplomacy to be explained by a need to overcome Irish rivals, especially the Butlers? And who killed the ninth Earl, said to have been slain by his own people? The place of the murder, Rathkeale, is agreed in *Annals of the Four Masters* and Russell: "The Earl of Desmond was treacherously slain by his own people at Rathgaela, at the instigation of John, his own brother. John and the other perpetrators of the murder were banished by Maurice, son of the Earl" (*Four Masters*, 1487).

Maurice, known as *Bacach*, or *the Lame*, succeeded his father about the time that Lambert Simnel, the first of the royal pretenders, landed in Ireland, which was in 1487. The second Yorkist pretender, Perkin Warbeck, landed in Munster in 1491 and again in 1494. Both impostors represented themselves as heirs to Edward IV, and on both occasions *the Lame* Earl made them welcome. He saw Perkin Warbeck as a possible conduit of men and arms from Burgundy for his struggle with the Butlers. Perhaps sensing that this was Maurice's use for Warbeck, King Henry decided against over-reacting and, still nervous of his throne, he opened negotiations with Maurice.

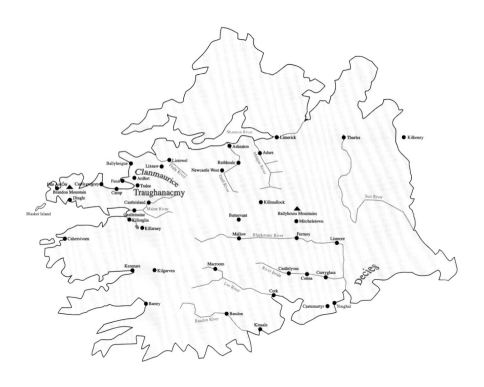

Map of sixteenth-century Munster: select physical features

[1] Paul MacCotter, "Lordship and Colony in Anglo-Norman Kerry", in *J.K.A.H.S.* 2004, p.41.

[2] Ibid., p.48.

[3] Mary Agnes Hickson, from the *Kerry Evening Post*, quoted in Kelly, Lucid, O'Sullivan, *Blennerville, Gateway to Tralee's Past*, Tralee 1989, pp. 202-203.

[4] Shanid is the broken ruin of the family's original fortification still to be seen near the village of Shanagolden, situated in the western barony of Co. Limerick that joins the northern barony of Kerry.

[5] In the 1940s, while preparing his book *In the Kingdom of Kerry*, Richard Hayward was shown "fifteen arch-frames of the old cloisters".

[6] "Some Old Tralee Notes", in *J.K.A.H.S.* 1997, pp.82-89, p.87.

[7] Ibid.

[8] John Bradley, "The Medieval Towns of Kerry", in *North Munster Antiquarian Journal*, 1986, pp.28-39, p.31.

[9] An error to this effect appeared in my *Pocket History of Kerry*; the Gaelic clans fought on both sides at Callan.

[10] Rev. James Graves, "The Earls of Desmond, Unpublished Geraldine Documents", in *J.R.S.A.I.*, 1869, pp. 459-559, p. 462. The story appears first in Thomas Russell's *Relation of the FitzGeralds of Ireland, written in the County of Clare 22 Oct. 1638*, in *J.H.A.A.I.* 1868-9, later in Dominic O'Daly, *The Rise, Increase and Exit of the Geraldines, Earls of Desmond*.

[11] Dominic O'Daly, *Geraldines, Earls of Desmond*, translated by C.P. Meehan, Dublin 1878, p.39.

[12] Thomas Johnson Westropp (1860-1922), "The Desmond Castle Newcastle West, Co. Limerick", in *J.R.S.A.I.*, 1909/1910, reprint 1983, p.44.

[13] *Calendar of Documents, Ireland, 1285-1292* (London 1879), p. 107; 28 April 1286.

[14] Ibid.

[15] *C.D.I., 1293-1301* (London 1881), 4 June 1298, 19 March 1300.

[16] MacCotter, *Lordship*, p.51.

[17] Quoted also in Anthony M. McCormack, *The Earldom of Desmond 1463-1583, the Decline and Crisis of a Feudal Lordship* (Dublin 2005), p. 47.

[18] J. J. Gilbert, *History of the Viceroys of Ireland* (Dublin 1865), pp. 307-8; Thomas Moore, whose father came from Kerry (we think Moyvane), used the episode as the inspiration for one of his lesser known *Melodies*: "By the Feale's wave benighted / Not a star in the skies / To thy door by Love lighted / I first saw those eyes …" (*Desmond's Song*, in *Irish Melodies*).

[19] Mary F. Cusack, *A History of the Kingdom of Kerry*, 1871, edn. 1995, p. 124; *Kerry Evening Post*, 11 December 1895; a transcription of the Castleisland treaty is reproduced in K.W. Nicholls, "The FitzMaurices of Kerry", in *J.K.A.H.S.*, 1970, p. 40-41.

[20] Westropp, *The Desmond Castle Newcastle West*, p. 51-52.

[21] Gilbert, *Viceroys of Ireland*, p. 354; Mary Hickson, *Kerry Evening Post*, 20 September 1893. York serves a second term from 1454 when the Roses conflict has begun. He is descended from the earls of Ulster. His beautiful wife, Cicely Neville, is known as the *Rose of Raby*.

[22] Michael O'Cleary's *Book of Pedigrees*, in Canon Hayman, "The Geraldines of Desmond", in *Journal of the Archaelolgical Association of Ireland*, 1879-82, p. 227; Thomas Johnson Westropp, *J.R.S.A.I.*, 1903, p. 33.

[23] Declan Downey, "Irish-European Integration, The Legacy of Charles V", in Judith Devlin and Howard B. Clarke (eds.) *European Encounters, Essays in Memory of Albert Lovett* (Dublin 2002), pp. 97-117, p.102.

TWO
RE-OCCUPATION, PLANTATION

I. REIGN OF HENRY VIII,
THE PROTESTANT REFORMATION AND THE COURT PAGE

During the reign of the second Tudor, Henry VIII, a powerful Earl of Desmond protected the Dominican Abbey of Tralee against the Dissolution policy then being implemented. The path to power for this Earl, James FitzJohn (r.1540-1558), involved murder and overthrow, and from it we trace the eventual downfall of the earldom; but from the early 1540s he used his considerable influence to protect the abbeys, not only in Kerry, but in Limerick and Youghal as well.

When the *Lame* Earl died in 1520 he had been in power for thirty-three years and seen the first eleven years of the reign of Henry VIII. His successor was James, eleventh Earl. By the time James succeeded, Martin Luther had defied the Pope by nailing his ninety-five theses on the church door at Wittenberg. Shortly after, Henry VIII renounced his allegiance to Rome in pursuit of his desire to divorce Catherine, his Spanish Queen, aunt of the powerful Charles V, Holy Roman Emperor and King of Spain. As Henry worked to detach Earl James from any European intrigues, the centre of intrigue had by now moved from Burgundy south to the court of Emperor Charles. The Emperor was Charles the Bold's great-grandson, and his prestige became greatly enhanced as a result of his defeat of the French at Pavia, northern Italy, in 1525.[24] Earl James sent his ambassadors from Dingle to meet those of the Emperor, and later the Emperor's ambassadors journeyed to Dingle where they signed the Treaty of Dingle in 1529, which granted the emigrant Irish the graces and privileges of subjects throughout the vast empire of Charles V. That same year Earl James was assassinated. Some attributed the deed to agents of King Henry.

In 1536 the Irish Parliament passed the Act of Supremacy imposing a Protestant oath on all office holders. In Dublin and the regions the dissolution of the monasteries began, inaugurating a wholesale transfer of monastic property. At this moment the Desmond earldom seemed to become the scene of fratricidal struggle. Earl James's successor was his aged uncle, Thomas, and Earl Thomas wished to secure his grandson's succession when he died. The grandson, another James, was raised at King Henry's court and became known as the *Court Page*; but when Earl Thomas died in 1534 the earldom became the scene of such bitter struggle that it embroiled all the major lordships of Munster. There were representations to Henry on the part of the late Earl's brother, John, and such was John's power that he became the *de facto* thirteenth Earl; but when he soon followed his brother to the grave, the claim to the earldom devolved on his son, James FitzJohn. When the Court Page appeared in Munster he was murdered by FitzJohn's brother, Maurice, known as *the Firebrand*.

James FitzJohn was the direct beneficiary of the murder of the Court Page, becoming as a result the 14th Earl of Desmond. He now began to assist the dissolution of the monasteries in Munster, and for his reward he gained official recognition as Earl, submitting in February 1541 to the new Lord Deputy, Sir Anthony St Leger.[25] Mary Hickson believed that, if instead of recognising FitzJohn, the English had sent him and his father to the Tower of London for the rest of their lives, Munster and the earldom (and England itself) would have been spared the disaster that befell both countries in the reign of FitzJohn's successor and heir. Dominican historian Dominic O'Daly agreed: "Alas! This horrid act was the first step to the ruin of the glorious family of the Geraldines".[26]

 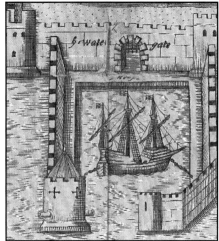

Ships at Youghal, from *Pacata Hibernia*

But credit must be given FitzJohn. At the time of his submission to St Leger he intended the protection of abbeys like Holy Cross in Tralee. Knowing how well his ancestors had endowed the religious orders, he made important and successful interventions to protect the houses which were at that moment being considered for dissolution, notably the Dominicans in Limerick city and the Dominicans and Franciscans of Youghal.[27] The Protestant Reformation would eventually penetrate Kerry, but there is no evidence that Tralee was affected this early, and for now the churches of Tralee, including Holy Cross, were safe. In the words of a recent historian, "all sources of annual income or revenue to their houses were restored to the Dominicans by royal consent", and "with the added generous financial support of the Earl, the Desmonds began to restore and repair some houses which had been sold or leased to laymen". On the list was Tralee.[28] Having accepted the Reformation and changed his religious allegiance,

FitzJohn reverted to Catholicism before his death.[29] Brother Michael O'Cleary recorded his death in his *Book of Pedigrees*: "James, son of John, son of Thomas, that is, the great Earl of Desmond, died on the 27 of the month of October, Thursday exactly, and he was buried in Tralee after victory from the Devil and from the world, 1558."[30] Other sources place his resting place at the Franciscan friary of Askeaton. Writing in the *Annals of the Four Masters*, Brother O'Cleary stated that James FitzJohn's loss "was woful to his country, for there was no need to watch cattle, or close doors from Dun-caoin, in Kerry, to the green-bordered meeting of the three waters" (a reference to the Rivers Barrow, Nore and Suir of East Munster and Leinster).

2. First Desmond Rebellion: Palatinate to Presidency

Queen Elizabeth succeeded to power in 1558, the same year as the new Earl, Garrett, or Gerald, and during her reign England pursued vigorously the subjugation of the South of Ireland. Elizabeth herself favoured a moderate policy, but an insurrection against Spanish rule in the Netherlands was suppressed with great ruthlessness by the Duke of Alva, and English privateers attacked Spanish vessels returning with gold from the Caribbean. This set of circumstances increased the likelihood that the southern Irish coastline would become the first landfall in any Spanish counter-attack, on which occasion the campfires of England's enemies would light up the headlands of West or South Kerry.

O'Cleary tells us that Gerald was fourteen years of age at the death of his father.[31] Unlike his father, James FitzJohn, he adhered to the old religion; unlike him, he received none of his father's government appointments; and he seemed to inherit none of his father's impressive personal attributes in diplomacy or the leadership of men. Worsted in an affray with the Butlers in border territory at Affane in 1565, probably in the course of reclaiming Decies, he suffered permanent injury to his hip and was brought from the field on a stretcher, and later to the Tower of London as a prisoner.

In his absence, his Captain (and cousin), James FitzMaurice FitzGerald, launched the first Desmond rebellion, provoked by the arrival of certain English adventurers in Munster in 1568-70. What do we know of FitzMaurice? He was the son of Maurice the Firebrand who murdered the Court Page, and he seems to have inherited something of his father's propensity for summary physical action. But there the similarity ends. Russell, the historian of the Desmond earls, wrote the following in the 1630s: FitzMaurice was "a brave and gallant gentleman, witty, learned, impassionate, circumspect, active, generous deuoute (devout), subtill, and quick of apprehension, eloquent, of a high and aduenturous polliticke and dissembling mind; too forward and apt to trauaile, to take great paynes, and to endure thirst, cold and hunger …". He was *not* much given to wine drinking (the delights of "Bacchus").[32]

The Elizabethan adventurers (Sir Peter Carew, Sir Humphrey Gilbert and Sir Warham St Leger among the better known), knowing of the Earl's imprisonment, anticipated the confiscation of his great inheritance. They fixed their attention first on Ormond (not Desmond) territory, which is why the resulting rebellion took place beyond the eastern frontier of Desmond's earldom, most notably in the barony of Idrone, in Carlow, where Carew had an old family claim. Yet the consequences for the Desmond earldom, including the town of Tralee, were catastrophic. The Irish counter-attack was led by James FitzMaurice FitzGerald, who allied with the brothers of the Earl of Ormond to expel the new arrivals, sending at the same time for international aid. The Earl's wife, Eleanor, suspecting FitzMaurice of wishing to supplant the Earl, corresponded with the Queen to gain her husband's release, all the while attempting to collect what rents she could to sustain him in prison.

Eleanor, Countess of Desmond, who later married O'Connor Sligo.
This is their tomb in Sligo Abbey.

Having waged terrible war on the English settlements in the East of Munster, FitzMaurice repeated the campaign with impressive victories in West Limerick and North Kerry. In 1569 he dispatched the Geraldine archbishop of Cashel, Maurice FitzGibbon, to Europe as his envoy. The Archbishop went first to Spain where he presented a memorial to Philip II. Meanwhile, Sir Henry Sidney had arrived as Lord Deputy with the task of defeating FitzMaurice. He went first to the relief of the eastern settlers, before turning round to concentrate on the strategic town of

Kilmallock, which he recovered. He left Sir Humphrey Gilbert in charge of Kilmallock as he himself proceeded into West Limerick and North Kerry where considerable support had accrued to James FitzMaurice, in the forms of MacCarthy Mór (Killarney), Roche (Fermoy), the Knight of Glin, and O'Brien of Thomond (Bunratty). There was terrible violence and counter-violence in the two campaigns. Gilbert, following Sidney into West Limerick and North Kerry, reported that he (Gilbert) spared nobody and no castle that did not submit to him.

John Derricke's image of Sir Henry Sidney departing Dublin

In 1570 Sidney abolished the Earl's palatinate of Kerry, inaugurating at the same time the Presidency of Munster. FitzMaurice submitted to Sidney at Kilmallock but later departed the country for Europe. In a strategic move, the English released Gerald from the Tower and permitted him to return to Ireland.

3. MASACARE AT DÚN AN ÓIR: THE LAST GERALDINE EARL OF TRALEE CASTLE

James FitzMaurice FitzGerald returned in July 1579 with a small force paid for out of Papal funds; he was accompanied by the English Jesuit, Dr Nicholas Sanders; they landed at Smerwick in the far west of the Dingle Peninsula:

"The Traitor upon Saturday last came out of his ship. Two friars bearing ensigns, & a bishop with a crozier staff & his mitre precede James Fitzmaurice. He has two vessels of 60 tons & four barks. He makes fires on the high hills and looks for more ships."[33]

FitzMaurice made his way inland, but was killed some miles outside the city of Limerick on the road east towards Cashel. The pressure was now on the Earl. Gerald's enemies had tried for years to force his hand, and by now his followers were seceding in droves to his brother Sir John of Desmond as the more effective commander. Sir John is believed to have led the band that murdered the two government officials, Davells and Carter, in their beds at an inn in Tralee shortly after the Smerwick landing. In November 1579, in an episode that defies rational explanation, Gerald sacked his own town of Youghal. Thereafter he was considered a rebel.

Two attacks were launched on Kerry by government forces in 1580. The first (Archdeacon Rowan's "The Black Earl's Raid" in his *Kerry Magazine*) was a joint operation in late March led by Ormond (Black Tom) and Lord Deputy Pelham. Pelham took the coastal route to Tralee through West Limerick while Ormond proceeded towards Newcastle. They communicated by the fires that marked their progress, burning homesteads and granaries. When they joined up at Shanid (near Shanagolden) they butchered four hundred people who had sought refuge in the woods. At Glin, the Lord of Lixnaw came in and surrendered. They proceeded to Tralee via the mouth of the Viall (Feale) river, and on 29 March Pelham recorded their arrival:

"All the country between the Earl's house of the Island and Tralighe was burnt by the rebels, and all the houses at Tralighe burnt and the castles razed, saving the abbey, a very convenient place for a garrison … I determined to leave there one band of horsemen and 300 footmen under Sir William Stanlie."[34]

Did they really push far into the Dingle Peninsula? Pelham seems to have wheeled around and gone to assist the siege of Carrigafoyle castle, where Ormond joined him on 27 March. The State Papers for the month of August refer to the skirmishes of the Queen's garrison of Kilmallock as it pursued the Earl's brother, Sir John of Desmond. A general pardon was issued to all rebels – with the exception of the Earl. The Countess, Eleanor, pleaded with the government for mercy.

The second and better known advance of the English into the Dingle Peninsula took place in November 1580, by which time Lord Grey de Wilton had replaced Pelham as Lord Deputy. Since the landing and subsequent death of FitzMaurice, Sir William Winter had been cruising off the coast hoping to intercept any new enemy force. Dr Sanders, FitzMaurice's Jesuit ally still at large, had been promising just such a second landing, though the Earl was being cursed by the ordinary people whenever they encountered him. Finally, a force of two hundred Spaniards and Italians came ashore near the same spot where FitzMaurice had landed over a year before: Dún an Óir. These new arrivals were massacred to the last man by a force led by Lord Grey de Wilton, with the participation of Edward Denny and (possibly) Walter Raleigh. The following account of the massacre is quoted in the *Kerry Archaeological Magazine* 1914-1916. Lord Grey writes to the Queen:

> "The same afternoone, 7th Nov. 1580, we landed our artillerie and munition; in the evening we fell to our worke … and planted two colverins with which next morning according upon daie we saluted them, and they for an hour or two as full requited us, until two of their best pieces at last taken away, they had not on that side but muskets and hackebusses to answer us, which with good heate plyed us with. The day so spent, at night we falle to agayne, and by morning brought our trench within 5 score of their ditch. This night they gave four sallies to have beaten our labourers from their work, and gave them vollies very gallantly, but were as gallantly set in againe by Ned Dennye and his company, who had this night the watch. Noo sooner daie peeped but they played very hotly upon us; yet, as God would, for a good time without hurte, till unhappily good John Cheke, too carelessly advancing himself to looke over the trench, struck on the hede, tumbled down at my feet, dead."

In desperation the Earl conducted a correspondence with the Pope to encourage another invasion from Catholic Europe.[35] It was too late. He was hunted down and finally killed on 11 November 1583 at Glenageenta, near Ballymacelligott, after a great manhunt that had drained his fragile physique and his remaining dignity. Yet even at the end he was not spared:

> "The Earl was most of this year accompanied by only two or three horsemen, and a Priest, with which retinue he was met in September, by some of the Lord Roche's men, and surrounded, but breaking through them, he escaped; the Priest fell into their hands, being poorly mounted, and was sent to the Earl of Ormond, to whom he related the great misery the Earl was in, lurking in corners for fear of being taken, and that he had his only relief from Goran Mac-Swiney, a Captain of Gallowglasses then under protection; who being soon after killed, and the Earl having taken a prey of cattle, was pursued to Kerry, near the side of a mountain, where there was a glin, and in it a little grove, through which one of the pursuers observed a fire not far off; one of the company on this information being sent to learn who was there, upon his return informed them, there were five or six people in an old house; whereupon they determined to attack them, and entering it found only an old man, the others being fled; when one Daniel Kelly (who was afterwards hanged at Tyburn) but for the present rewarded by Queen Elizabeth, almost cut off his arm with his sword, and repeating the blow over his head, the old man cried out, desiring them to save his life, for that he was Earl of Desmond. Kelly upon this desisted; but the effusion of blood causing him to grow faint, and being unable to travel, he bad him prepare for death; and on the 11th

of November 1583, struck off his head; which was sent by the Earl of Ormond into England, for a present to the Queen, who caused it to be fixed upon London bridge, and his body after 8 weeks hiding, was buried in the chapel of Killanamana near Arnegragh, in the County of Kerry. Thus fell this unhappy Earl, stiled in history, *Ingens Rebellibus Exemplar*; and thus says Hooker, a noble race and antient family descended out of the loins of Princes, is now for treasons and rebellions utterly extinguished and overthrown."[36]

The old man cried out, desiring them to save his life.

His body was brought to the little graveyard of Kilnanaimh among the Sliabh Luachra hills.

Artist Julia Sexton

4. TRALEE DESTROYED:
SIR EDWARD DENNY AND THE MUNSTER PLANTATION

The stricken condition of the town is conveyed by the Desmond Survey: "(Tralee) was formerly a well-inhabited borough, with a castle and edifices in it, formerly well and fully repaired … now ruined and broken … Several other burgages and gardens there, being in the streets or broadways called the Burgess-street and Great Castle-street, and others within and without the said town, now prostrated …". Not only Tralee, but all of Munster lay in ruins: "The wasteness of this province is so universal for want of people that it will be very long before the inhabitants shall regain any ability of living".[37]

Parliament enacted two bills of attainder in 1586 after which the earldom could be carved up among the planters. One of the commissioners of the plantation Survey, Sir Valentine Browne, became one of the leading Kerry planters, his seat at Molahiffe some ten miles east of Tralee. Sir Thomas Norreys held temporary possession of the Great Castle of Tralee "and another old Castle near adjoining called the Countess Castel, alias the Newe Manor", as well as Holy Cross and the house of the Knights Hospitaller.[38] All of these possessions were transferred to Sir Edward Denny, the *Ned Denny* who had so distinguished himself at the massacre at Dún an Óir. The extent of the Denny estate in and around Tralee was 6000 acres.

It would be difficult to imagine anybody better connected than Denny. His father, Sir Anthony Denny, was Henry VIII's executor and the recipient of Waltham Abbey at the dissolution of the monasteries. When the king could no longer sign his name, Sir Anthony was at hand with a stamp bearing the King's signature; and when death was near, it was Denny who advised Henry to prepare to meet his Maker. Sir Edward maintained his father's court affiliations, and when he married, it was to Margaret Edgcumbe, a maid of honour to Queen Elizabeth.[39] Sir Edward's aunt on his mother's side was the mother of the famous courtiers, half-brothers Sir Walter Raleigh and Sir Humphrey Gilbert, whom Denny had joined on a failed expedition to North America after Gilbert had received a charter to found a colony. Raleigh and Gilbert and some of the leading *undertakers* of the Munster Plantation were natives of the Devon and Cornwall peninsula of western England; the mothers of Raleigh, Gilbert and Denny – the Champernowne sisters – came from Modbury in Devon. On his father's side, Sir Edward Denny was connected by marriage with Sir Francis Walsingham, a hawkish figure in the quartet that surrounded the Queen, with the powerful Earl of Leicester, Sir Christopher Hatton and the moderate Lord Burghley (Sir William Cecil).[40] The sister of Leicester (Robert Dudley) was the wife of the Irish Lord Deputy of the 1560s and 1570s, Sir Henry Sidney. Their famous son, Sir Philip Sidney, poet and ambassador to the Protestant League in Europe, married Denny's first cousin, Frances Walsingham, and corresponded with Denny. Sir Philip's sister, Mary, the famous Countess of Pembroke, patron of writers (including her brother), was the wife of Henry Herbert, second Earl of Pembroke, second cousin of Denny's fellow-undertaker in the Tralee district, Sir William Herbert of St. Julian's, in Wales.

Sir Edward Denny & his wife Margaret Edgcumbe
© Victoria and Albert Museum.

Denny, as we have seen, had come to Ireland with Lord Grey de Wilton (yet another family connection) in time to participate in the massacre at Dún an Óir in November 1580. As part of the Plantation which followed, Denny received Tralee Castle and surrounding district from the President of Munster, Sir Thomas Norreys, who himself became the occupant of the Desmond Castle at Mallow. Norreys announced to Lord Burghley that he "had delivered Tralee to Mr Dennye".[41] According to Denny family tradition, the estate extended from Liscahane to Gleann na nGealt (*Glen of the Mad Men*) at Camp, a circle of territory around Tralee Bay.

Denny's connection with Walsingham and Raleigh would tend to place him on the hawkish side of government policy. On the other hand, the Dennys were neighbours of the moderate Burghley. When the Welsh settler Sir William Herbert arrived to occupy the Earl's manor and castle at Castleisland, he brought some opposing ideas about how to cultivate the Irish. Herbert favoured education and religious conversion, even suggesting the translation of the Bible into Irish. Denny was more the man of action, often absent from Tralee. He was absent in the first week of September 1588 when two vessels of the Spanish Armada appeared in "a small creek nere to Tralee", one of them with a cargo of twenty tons of "sack" (white wine). Twenty sailors were captured and when Sir Edward returned from Cork he had them all hanged. Herbert complained to Walsingham that Denny had kept treasure from the vessels for himself.[42] How did Denny view the continued existence of Holy Cross? Historian Annie Rowan wrote: "It is worthy of remark that the inspectors were careful to mark as 'respected', or 'respited' such church lands as they were unable to survey or value. Also, it is well to remember that some of these 'respited' Desmond monasteries were afterwards (under the rule of Elizabeth and the protection of the Dennys) resuscitated."[43]

Other near neighbours of Denny included Robert Blennerhassett and his aged father Thomas. They came from Flimby, in Cumberland, and occupied the old castle of Ballycarty, a few miles east of the town. The Blennerhassetts were tenants of Denny, to whom they paid the annual tribute of "one red rose". A little further to the east there was Valentine Browne, whose seignory was centred on Molahiffe, Firies. The Brownes later acquired land around Killarney where they moved to live. The other great Killarney family, Herbert, moved from Castleisland to settle at Killarney as recently as the eighteenth century when one of the family inherited the estate of MacCarthy Mór.

Sir Walter Raleigh

The Munster Plantation is inseparable from the name of the most famous Munster planter of all, the poet and explorer Sir Walter Raleigh who was granted an enormous estate out of confiscated property in modern counties Cork and Waterford. Did Raleigh participate in the massacre at Dún an Óir? Some think not: the legend that he did probably rests on his undeniable support for extreme policies to quell the native Irish, specifically his wish that somebody like his half-brother Sir Humphrey Gilbert could be put in charge to replace the like of Ormond, Ormond being too well affiliated with the native Irish and with Catholics generally to see through the task of subjugating Munster effectively.

Black Thomas Butler, 10th Earl of Ormond.
Butler territory bordered that of the earl of Desmond in the East of Munster. Both earls claimed rights at sea, Desmond claiming the "wrecks of ships and storms" from Valentia to Beale in Clanmaurice, and the "presage of all wines" imported "at Dingle, Bantry, Smerwick and Ardecanny" (Desmond Survey).

Dingle did not escape in the destruction of the earldom. The town's architecture had a distinctively Spanish character. A charter was granted in 1585 to help with "the restoration of their ruinous and decayed estate through the late rebellion there", together with a grant of £300 sterling "towards the performance of so good a work as the walling of their town", the repayment of which was to be £20 per annum out of the import of wine at the port.[44] The borough came under the control of the FitzGeralds, Knights of Kerry, in circumstances that are not entirely clear. A visitor to Dingle in 1589, the Earl of Cumberland, en route to the Azores, heard that the destruction of the town was to be blamed on the Earl of Desmond's forces. "The Castle and all the houses in the town, save four, were won, burnt, and ruinated by the Earl of Desmond. These four houses fortified themselves against him, and withstood him and all his power, so that he could not win them. There yet remaineth a thick stone wall that passeth overthwart the midst of the street; which was a part of their fortifications. ... The town is again somewhat repaired; but in effect there remains but the ruins of the former town."[45]

5. HUGH O'NEILL'S WAR: THE SÚGAN EARL AND FLORENCE MACCARTHY BURN TRALEE

The Plantation of Munster was overthrown and the Tralee settlers forced to flee to Cork when Hugh O'Neill, Earl of Tyrone, brought his war against Elizabeth to the South of Ireland. The year was 1598, and Tyrone had two southern allies, the Súgan Earl of Desmond, and Florence MacCarthy Prince of Carbery who had married the daughter of MacCarthy Mór of Killarney.

The Súgan, or *Straw* Earl (James FitzThomas FitzGerald), claimed that the late *Rebel*, Gerald, was never the rightful Earl. The rightful Earl was the Súgan's father, Thomas of Conna (a fortress overlooking the river Bride near the Cork border with Waterford), who was the first son of the mighty 14th Earl: the *Rebel* Earl was but a younger step-brother of this Thomas of Conna.

We return to the plight of the Tralee settlers. In October 1598 Ormond wrote to the Privy Council that "all the English of Kerry have abandoned it". The Mayor of Cork complained to the Privy Council that the Kerry settlers "came to this city for their refuge, after being rifled and spoiled, their women and children of all their goods, yea of the very clothes from their backs".[46] From Cork, at about the beginning of November 1598, the settlers (as "yor. highnes poore distressed subjects of the countie of Kerrie in Ireland") petitioned the Queen directly, suggesting that she appoint Sir Edward Denny governor of a single County hitherto divided into the Counties of Kerry and Desmond. The new "pretended Earle of Desmond" (the Súgan) was the instigator of the "irrecuperable miseries (including) the loss of their husbandes, children, families and goods by the outrageous murthers and spoiles in those partes dailie comytted".[47] Their nearest saviour was Sir Thomas Norreys at Mallow, but he was too far away to be of any use, which is why they urged the appointment of Denny.

Sir George Carew commanded the Queen's forces, who held Castlemaine, though not Dingle where "William FitzGerald, alias the Knight of Kerry, one of the principal traitors in those parts ... compelled (the inhabitants) to surrender unto him all their estates". FitzMaurice of Lixnaw had joined the insurrection, together with "all the freeholders and inhabitants of Kerry", all urged on by their "papistical priests".[48]

Denny died in February 1599 "of a sickness taken in his country's service" at the comparatively young age of fifty-two. His town lay in ruins: a survey two decades later could still record "a fair house built in the Abbey of Tralee by Sir Edward Denny and fifty other houses built by tenants, all destroyed in the time of the rebellion".[49] He had complained to the Queen that the rebels had even destroyed his stud of thoroughbred horses. Eighteen months after Denny's death Carew sent Sir Charles Wilmot to Tralee, Wilmot having recently taken Listowel Castle:

> "(Wilmot) went to view Tralee, which was Sir Edward Denny's house, and now utterly defaced, nothing being left unbroken but a few old vaults; and as they were breaking of them, he came so suddenly upon the bonnaughts appointed by James FitzThomas to see that work being perfected ..."[50]

Sir George Carew

A wealth of Dominican archives must have suffered in 1598 and again in the contest between the Súgan (James FitzThomas) and Carew; and the repeated destruction of the town postponed the reoccupation of the Castle by the Denny family, on account of which they constructed a residence in the Elizabethan style at Carrignafeela, near Ballymacelligott.

Sir Richard Boyle, later first Earl of Cork, who came to Ireland with Carew, might usefully be introduced at this point. His great estate on the Bride and Blackwater rivers was acquired originally by Sir Walter Raleigh after the suppression of the Desmond Rebellion, but while Raleigh languished in the Tower of London, Carew suggested to Boyle, as one of the rising young soldiers in his Munster army, that he could do worse than acquire Raleigh's estate. This, Boyle did. Boyle married Joan Apsley, and when she died young he married the daughter of Geoffrey Fenton, Secretary to the Irish government, with whom he had a large family. Their descendants included the Dukes of Devonshire. Boyle acknowledged that it was his Apsley inheritance that set him on the road to great landed wealth, including property in West Kerry owned by his Boyle descendants, the earls of Cork. Part of his Apsley inheritance was the district of Hospital and Awney (Knockainy) in Co. Limerick, which contained a preceptory of the Knights Hospitaller from which a daughter house in Tralee was founded: Teampall on tSoluis.

THE ELIZABETHAN DENNYS

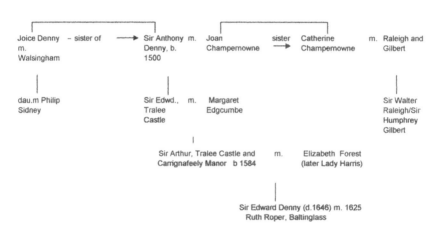

[24] McCormack, *The Earldom of Desmond*, p. 64.

[25] Brendan Bradshaw, *The Dissolution of the Religious Orders in Ireland under Henry VIII* (Cambridge 1974), p.148.

[26] Mary Hickson, *The Kerry Evening Post*, 15 October 1893; O'Daly, p.57.

[27] Bradshaw, *Dissolution*, p.150.

[28] Thomas S. Flynn, OP, *The Irish Dominicans 1536-1641*, 1993, p.45.

[29] For James FitzJohn's changes of religion, see Mairtin Ó Corrbuí, *Kenry, The Story of a Barony in County Limerick*, Dundalk 1975.

[30] Canon Hayman, "The Geraldines of Desmond", *J.H.A.A.I.*, 1881, p.413.

[31] Hayman, "Geraldines of Desmond", p.413.

[32] Thomas Russell's *Relation of the FitzGeralds of Ireland*, 1638.

[33] *Cal. S. P.*, 1571-1585, James Golde, Tralee, to the Mayor of Limerick, 22 July 1579.

[34] *Cal. Carew Mss.* 1575-88, Pelham to the Lords of the Council in England, 29 March 1580, p.237.

[35] Margaret MacCurtain, *The Fall of the House of Desmond, J.K.A.H.S. 1975*, p.28-44, p.39.

[36] Charles Smith, *The Antient and Present State of the County and City of Cork* (2 vols. 1750), vol. ii.

[37] *Cal. S. P.* 1574-1585, 31 March 1585, Thomas Norreys to Lord Burghley.

[38] Mary Hickson, "The Knights of St John in Kerry", in J.R.S.A.I., 1889, pp. 184-191, p. 185; *The Irish Fiants of The Tudor Sovereigns*, vol. 3 *Queen Elizabeth*, no. 5043. Denny was also granted Lislaughtin "and the circuit of the house of Franciscan Friars of Lislaughtin, in Iraught I Knoghor's country" (Fiant 5177).

[39] The Edgcumbes were an Anglo-Norman family long settled in Devon and Cornwall. Sir Richard Edgcumbe, sent over as ambassador to Ireland at the time of the pretender Lambert Simnel, appears to have been an ancestor.

[40] Rev. Sir H.L.L. Denny, "Biography of Sir Edward Denny, Knight Banneret, of Bishop's Stortford, Herts., Gentleman of the Privy Chamber to Queen Elizabeth, Governor of Kerry and Desmond", in *Transactions of the East Herts. Archaeological Society*, vol. 2 part 3, (originally prepared for the *Hertfordshire Dictionary of Biography*), appeared subsequently in the *Kerry Evening Post* of 22 and 26 September 1906.

[41] *Old Kerry Records*, Series 1, p.135, quoting the *Kerry Magazine*, September 1854.

[42] Brendan G. Carthy *The Surrender of an Armada Vessel near Tralee; an Exploration of the State Papers, J.K.A.H.S.* 1990, p. 91-93.

[43] *K.E.P.*, 30 May 1891.

[44] *Calendar of the Patent and Close Rolls of Chancery Ireland from the 18th to the 45th of Queen Elizabeth*, James Morrin (ed.), vol. 2, p.105.

[45] Edward Wright, Mathematician, *The Voyage of the Earl of Cumberland to the Azores in 1589*, in Arber's *English Garner: Voyages and Travels*, vol. II, 1903.

[46] *Cal. S. P Reign of Elizabeth*, January 1598-March 1599.

[47] The original letter to the Queen from the Tralee settlers is in the possession of Sir Anthony Denny; a transcription copy appeared in *Notes and Queries*, 8 September 1923.

[48] *Cal. S. P, Reign of Elizabeth Jan. 1598-March 1599*, Norreys to Privy Council, 9 Dec. 1598, p. 400.

[49] Victor Treadwell, *The Irish Commission of 1622* (Irish Manuscripts Commission 2006), p. 491; Robert Dunlop, "An Unpublished Survey of the Plantation of Munster in 1622", *J.R.S.A.I.*, vol. 54, 1924, part 2, pp.128-146, p.136.

[50] *Cal. S. P*, Sir George Carew to Privy Council, Cork, 25 August 1600.

THREE
CHARTER

1. REIGN OF JAMES I (1603-1625): TRALEE GETS ITS CHARTER

"The town was incorporated by a charter of the 10th of Jas. I. under the name of 'the Provost, Free Burgesses, and Commonalty of the Borough of Tralee', to consist of a provost, 12 burgesses and a commonalty."

(Samuel Lewis, *A Topographical Dictionary of Ireland*, London 1837)

King James I

The defining event of the reign of James I is the Plantation, or settlement, of the counties of Ulster in the North of Ireland. After the Spanish invasion had been thwarted at Kinsale, and before the Ulster Plantation, James had wished to capitalise on Spain's desire for peace. Philip III had replaced his warlike father on the Spanish throne, the Spanish commissioners arrived in London, and in 1604 a treaty was signed. To the perplexity of historians, the leaders of the Ulster revolt departed the province for exile in Europe, and this *Flight of the Earls* made possible the *Plantation* of the province. The situation did not augur well for Ireland's Catholics to whose dismay James seemed more eager to placate the powerful Puritan faction than the followers of his martyred mother, Mary Queen of Scots.

The principal purpose of the 1613 Charter[51] was to ensure the return of two MPs to the Irish Parliament in the King's support. Robert Blennerhassett and Humphrey Dethick, the first MPs, were burgesses of the corporation, and Robert Blennerhassett the town's first Provost. The Charter also recognised the corporation's role in local government. There were twelve burgesses (Arthur Denny included) and they met on the nativity of St John the Baptist to elect a Provost whose installation took place each 29 September, the Feast of St Michael the Archangel. It became known as Corporation Day. The new Provost took the Oath of Supremacy, the religious test that excluded the majority population of Catholics. The framework was in place for the governance of Tralee until the Municipal Reform Act of 1840.

Robert Blennerhassett had fled with the other settlers when the Plantation was overthrown by the Súgan Earl. In the 1613 Parliament he took the side of the King's deputy in a celebrated protest by the Catholic MPs against the nominated Speaker. In the words of the Carew Papers, under 18 May: "The Parliament having given their voices unto the election of Sir John Davies, the Papists cried No, and named Sir John Everard". On 27 May, Davies was ejected from the chair and Everard put in his place. There were concurrent protests from the Catholics about the King's instructions for the creation of the new corporations, and they demanded to see the king's letters on the matter. County Kerry MPs Daniel O'Sullivan of Dunloe and Stephen Rice of Ballinruddell (sic) supported the leader of the agitation, Daniel O'Brien of Carrigaholt, MP Co. Clare. (O'Brien was the future Viscount Clare, ancestor of many Kerry families, the most prominent of whom were the FitzGeralds, Knights of Kerry.) In the following year, 1614, King James responded formally to the Catholic protests, and their delegations: "The like never was heard of in France or Spain or other kingdom of Christendom". He condemned their assembly as unconstitutional, likewise their deputation, and what he termed their purpose to introduce the Pope: "You would have a visible body head of the Church over all the earth ...".[52]

Meanwhile, Arthur Denny was preoccupied with reconstruction. He succeeded his father at sixteen years of age on Sir Edward's death in 1599, and a few years later married Elizabeth

Forest, who, like her mother-in-law Margaret Edgcumbe, was a former lady in waiting to Queen Elizabeth. Arthur's immediate priority was to create a dwelling alternative to the ruined Castle of Tralee. A plantation Survey informs us that he constructed "one dwelling place for the chief Undertaker at Carrignefely (and) 79 houses and tenements, of which 32 are in the town of Tralee" (the others elsewhere in the seignory).[53] This temporary, long-forgotten Elizabethan mansion house of the Dennys lay in the parish of Ballymacelligott, some miles east of the town and close to the location of the Earl of Desmond's violent death. Funds continued scarce. In 1607 Arthur petitioned the King, "craving the remittal of certain arrears", his father having "lost his life and his cattle, goods, and benefit of his lands which he had".[54] Arthur sought remission of "the relief due upon his father's death and the arrears of rent since the beginning of the late wars until next Michaelmas following", also "that he might have the arrears and present growing rent due to the late Earl of Desmond from the burgesses of Tralee, amounting to the sum of eighteen marks …". The charges were waived: "The arrears are greater than by any likelihood can be paid in many years out of Mr. Denny's seignory, the same lying much waste ...[55]

Sir Arthur died young in 1619, and the Castle continued in a ruined state at the time of a plantation Survey in 1622.

2. RIDING THE CIRCUIT OF THE ABBEY: THE THIRD DENNY USURPS THE CHARTER

Arthur may have played a part in the rebuilding of the Castle, but the main work was undertaken by the third generation of Denny settlers, his son and heir Sir Edward (1605-1646), who is the incumbent at Tralee Castle for the turbulent reign of King Charles I (1625-49) that ends with the King's execution: "I finished this Great Castle of Tralee and came with my mother to live in it upon the 22 of December 1627." His wife, Ruth Roper, moved in later: "The 20th of November 1629, my wife and I began house-keeping in this greate castle."[56]

By an indenture made 10 May 1627 Sir Edward "granted to the Provost and Burgesses of Tralee the circuit and liberty of the Abbey, and all privileged places in the said Borough". A condition was attached: Sir Edward and his heirs would appoint a town clerk and have all the profits accruing to him.[57] Sir Edward granted the provost and burgesses the tolls and customs of Tuesday's weekly market, as well as those of the annual St James's Fair held in August. (The majority population paid tolls; freemen paid none.) It is by no means clear that these concessions were Sir Edward's to make, and it is more likely that we are seeing the usurpation of the Charter by the Denny family.

Sir Edward Denny (1605-1646)

Artist unknown. Sir Edward rebuilt Tralee Castle between the years 1615 and 1625. He gave the "the circuit and liberty of the Abbey" to the Corporation. He evacuated his wife and children from Tralee at the beginning of the Confederate war and sent them to his grandmother Margaret Edgcumbe at Bishop's Stortford. He became head of the family on the death, without male issue, of his father's first cousin, Sir Edward Denny, Baron Denny de Waltham and Earl of Norwich, in 1637. He died in 1646, predeceasing his grandmother.

Ruth Roper, Sir Edward's wife, was the daughter of Thomas, Viscount Baltinglass, described in the *Complete Peerage* as "a distinguished commander in the armies of Elizabeth and James". He appears to be the same individual who had come to Kerry to manage the Herbert estate at Castleisland for its absentee owner, and who had acquired near it some portion of the MacElligott estate not already granted to Chute.[58] Ruth Roper came with powerful family affiliations, and she would leave her name in a suburb of Tralee: Garry Ruth. Her cousins were the Sidneys: Sir Henry Sidney was that long-serving lord deputy of Queen Elizabeth's reign, whose son was Sir Philip Sidney, the much admired poet and soldier, friend and correspondent of the first Denny settler. Yet when Ruth's husband completed the work of reconstruction, it was a former Lady Denny, his mother, who continued to wield power in Tralee Castle. This was Elizabeth Forest: she remarried after Arthur's death, to Sir Thomas Harris, and this is the couple who wielded effective power at Tralee Castle in the turbulent days ahead.

In 1628, with England once again at war with Spain, the Irish agreed money subsidies with the government in return for what became known as the *Graces*, which, among other things, promised the security of those Irish lordships still at risk of royal confiscation. All that was needed was for these Graces to be ratified. But when Richard Boyle became one of the Lords Justices in 1629 there was going to be no progress on the issue of the Graces, only a renewed energy to enforce the recusancy fines and other disabilities against Catholics. In consequence, Boyle's actions further strengthened the alliance of the Old English (Anglo-Normans) and the native Irish. Historian Mary Hickson has written about a controversy involving Lady Harris and Boyle surrounding certain properties in Tralee, including Teampall an tSoluis. After the Desmond Wars the Desmond lands in and around Tralee, including "the Hospitall and Burgess lands of Tralye", were in the custody of Sir Thomas Norreys, the grantee of Mallow Castle, before being granted to Sir Edward Denny in 1587. Lady Harris, on behalf of her former husband Sir Arthur, and their children, fought to retain the Hospitaller property against Boyle. It was a long controversy, but we assume it had an amicable resolution in light of the marriage of Lady Harris's grandson by Arthur Denny to Lady Ellen Barry, Boyle's granddaughter, a generation or so later.[59]

There is no mention of a Dominican community in Tralee in the Order's own lists for 1622 and 1629, though priests may have survived individually or in scattered, informal communities.[60] The difficulties of the Catholic diocese may be inferred from the fact that Bishop Rickard O'Connell's appointment in 1611 remained nominal for many years, but eventually he felt sufficiently confident to found a seminary in Tralee for the formation of diocesan clergy, and he entered more fully into his episcopal powers when the Catholics throughout Ireland rebelled in 1641. Boyle's rule ended with the arrival of Wentworth as Lord Deputy in 1633, and then religious as well as laity looked forward to a milder regime for the exercise of their religion.

They rested their hopes on Wentworth because Wentworth set about enforcing the High Church policy of Bishop Laud who was as much the enemy of Puritans as of Catholics. However, as tensions continued to rise in England between the King and his subjects, the crisis in the royal finances dictated Wentworth's Irish policy; so the Graces were further postponed and the land titles of the Irish lordships were brought under renewed scrutiny, particularly those of Ormond and the Clanricarde Burkes of Connaught. Before Wentworth's arrival, the taxation of corporations had been kept low on account of the wars at the turn of the century. This changed with Wentworth, who also pursued a personal vendetta against Boyle and Boyle's wealth derived from the Church, and he famously compelled Boyle to relocate the tomb he had built for himself in St Patrick's Cathedral, Dublin.

Sir Richard Boyle, first Earl of Cork, and his wife Katherine Fenton

Before a new Parliament assembled in 1634, Wentworth interfered with the elections to try to arrange the return of supporters of the King. In that year Tralee again returned that old survivor from the Munster Plantation and the town's first Provost, Robert Blennerhassett, together with the outsider Sir Beverley Newcomen. The other boroughs, Ardfert and Dingle, as well as the County, returned Catholics, underlining the Protestant character of Tralee's representation at a time when Catholics, including Old English and Irish, constituted a powerful alliance in the Irish Parliament.[61]

By 1634 Robert Blennerhassett's son John (the *Capt. Hassett* of the coming Civil War) had acquired a wife in Martha Lynne, of Norhamptonshire, in the English Midlands. Martha's mother, a Forest, was a sister of Lady Harris, Arthur Denny's widow, of neighbouring Huntingdonshire. We may never know the part Lady Harris played in bringing over one of her own as a wife for her Tralee neighbour, but the match is indicative of how the Munster settlement prospered with the aid of some social engineering on the part of settlers' wives. Martha Lynne was present in 1635 at a Denny baptism: Sir Edward recorded in the Family *Diary* the name of "my cousin Martha Blennerhassett" as one of the sponsors of baby Elizabeth Denny, his and Ruth Roper's daughter.

3. CIVIL WAR 1642: SIEGE OF TRALEE AND ITS TWO CASTLES – THE BURNING OF THE TOWN

At the end of 1641, about five weeks after a great insurrection against the Ulster Plantation, rebel forces descended on Munster through the gaps in the Ballyhoura hills behind Kilmallock. A Scottish insurrection had preceded the Ulster revolt; it plunged England into civil war by bringing the Scots into alliance with their co-religionists, the Parliamentary extremists in London. In response to events in England and in Ireland, the Confederation of Kilkenny became the forum of the Irish Catholic alliance, and the seat of its military command.

Having penetrated the barrier of hills into North Cork, the Irish insurgents were joined by the forces of Roche and MacDonogh, and by the rebels of Limerick. In the first days of February 1642 the Lord President of Munster, Sir William St Leger, whose mansion at Doneraile was situated in the centre of the southern war theatre, assembled his Munster loyalists to confront the invaders. He had six hundred foot and three hundred horse, and his commanders included the Earl of Barrymore (David Barry), Sir Edward Denny and that redoubtable leader of the Munster Protestants, Lord Broghill, who was a son of Richard Boyle, as well as that other future commander of Oliver Cromwell's forces in Munster, Sir Hardress Waller – all of whom "most willingly and affectionately attended the President (St Leger)".[62] The army proceeded to Red Shard in the Ballyhouras but the anticipated battle with the united Irish of the Confederation of Kilkenny never materialised, and by February the Irish were laying siege to Mallow, where they were repulsed.[63] The Confederate Irish of Munster were led by Donogh MacCarthy, second Viscount Muskerry, whose principal castles were Blarney and Macroom. As the brother-in-law of Ormond, the King's representative, Muskerry might be expected to be with the President; but he was disgusted at the President's repressive actions, and by St Patrick's Day he had joined the Confederate Irish.

Before this, Sir Edward Denny, who was Governor of the fortress of Castlemaine, delivered up that place to Captain Thomas Spring (having received the order to do so from the Governor of Kerry, FitzMaurice), and went to Tralee to raise forces for St Leger. He quitted Tralee just before the new year with a hundred men, "taking with him his lady and children, whom he sent soon after to England to his grandmother, Margaret, Lady Denny, at Bishop's Stortford". His family remained there for the duration of the war.[64] Sir Edward made his stepfather, Sir Thomas Harris, and Peter White, Provost of Tralee, joint Governors of the two Castles of Tralee. The advance of the war into Kerry had been delayed by the geographical obstacles of those inhospitable hills just east of Killarney, but when the Irish took Castlemaine, all the English, to the number of about four hundred, fled to Tralee Castle. The town was taken and plundered on 15 February, but the Castle would hold out for many long months of siege. Rev. Devereux Spratt, tutor to Sir Edward Denny's children, was an eyewitness:

"I was Tutor to Sr Edward Denny's 3 sons. ... In Feb. 1641 (1642 in our calendar) it reached us, the whole County being up in Rebellion, and 2 companyes besieging us in 2 small Castles; where I saw ye miserable destruction of 100 and 20 men, women and children, by sword, famine, and many deseases, amongst whom fell my mother Elyzabeth, and my youngest brother Joseph, both which lyes interred there. ... After two months siege both castles were surrendered upon Artickles into ye hands of the Irish Rebbells. Then ye Lord removed me to Bally Begg Garrison, where I preached to the poor stript Protestants there. And passing thence to Ballingarry, an Island of the Shannon, I fell sicke of a feavor, out of which the Lord delivered me. Then having an opportunity I returned to Bally Begg, Captaine Ferretter being my Convoy, where I remained in the discharge of my calling till the English army came up to carry us of. At which time ye enemy burned booth ye Castle and Towne of Tralee, and twice set upon us in our march to Corke, but with ye power of God wee still beat them. Then at Corke I petitioned the Lord Inchaquen, who gave me a pass for England ..."[65]

Pierce Ferriter, from the far west of the Dingle peninsula was one of those who led the siege of Tralee Castle, which lasted until about 20 August. It surrendered on condition that those inside the Castle were allowed take refuge at Ballingarry, a fortress north of Causeway on the Shannon held by Colonel David Crosbie. Lord Inchiquin (O'Brien), St Leger's successor, reported that Crosbie:

"hath there relieved many Protestants especially about 200 who endured a long & hard siege at Tralee & were received by him & there kept about one month at his own charge until he had opportunity to send them unto the Lord Forbes his fleet then riding in the river of Shannon".[66]

The charismatic Ferriter was evidently a friend of the FitzMaurices lords Kerry. Lady Kerry in the absence of her husband, the Governor of Kerry, Patrick FitzMaurice, appealed to Ferriter to remain loyal, to no avail. Tralee Castle and the Short Castle, situated at the present Square, held out all summer, but after Sir Thomas Harris died from the effects of drinking bad water, the occupants became demoralised. During the siege, the Irish overran all of Co. Limerick and prepared to take the corporation towns of South Munster where men and supplies had failed to reach the beleaguered inhabitants; in addition, the President, St Leger, had died, and there were doubts surrounding the loyalties of his successor, Inchiquin. Then, against the tide of events, the English gained a famous victory over the Irish at Liscarrol, near Charleville, though Boyle's son, Lord Kinalmeaky, was killed in the battle. The two castles of Tralee capitulated at the end of August; a third, Ballybeggan Castle on the north-east of the town, commanded by Richard Exham, resisted successfully, and was relieved by a force from Cork in the following year.

The English of Munster were radicalised by the Cessation of 1643 agreed by the King with the Confederation through his Lord Lieutenant Ormond, and by the victories of the Parliamentarians in England at the battles of Marston Moor and Naseby. Sir Edward Denny did not live to witness the next phase: the transformation of the war under Cromwell, who was free to deal ruthlessly with Ireland from the ending of the Thirty Years War in Europe in 1648 and the execution of King Charles in the following year. Denny saw none of this new phase. Denny served only Ormond, sailing from Cork as the siege of his Castle in Tralee was in progress, cruising around the coast of Kerry seeking to encounter the Irish, and encountering them at a small affray in *Garri na Sassanach*, "the Englishmen's Garden", near Ballinaskelligs.[67] He died in 1646.

The sack of Cashel by Inchiquin, now prosecuting the war with vigour for the Parliamentarians, followed in 1647, then the overthrow of the Irish at the battle of Knocknanuss in North Cork. Cromwell landed in Dublin in 1649 and sacked Drogheda and Wexford. The south Munster towns (including the Boyle towns of Youghal and Bandon) revolted in his favour, and when he left Ireland he handed command to Broghill, Ludlow, Waller and the other Parliamentary generals, Inchiquin having by then gone over to the Confederate side. Broghill hanged the Catholic Bishop of Ross, Boetius MacEgan, after taking the town of Macroom in 1650. The way was clear to Kerry, and the final chapter of the war was played out at the siege of Ross Castle in 1652.

4. RECOVERY AND RESTORATION; CAPT. HASSET, MARTHA LYNNE AND THE BUILDING OF BALLYSEEDY

The Blennerhassetts of Ballycarty, including two sons of Capt. Hassett and Martha Lynne, and Capt. Hassett himself, participated in the final phase of the war after Capt. Hassett's contemporary, Sir Edward Denny, had died, sharing in the Cromwellian victory while the Denny heir, Sir Arthur, and his many brothers and sisters, remained at Bishop's Stortford. This meant that the Blennerhassett estate was protected from the subsequent confiscations, while the Denny estate lay exposed. Martha Lynne, Capt. Hassett's fascinating wife, came from Southwick Hall, in Northamptonshire, which was not far from Oliver Cromwell's home, in neighbouring Huntingdonshire. In Huntingdonshire, Morborne was the home of Elizabeth Forest, Sir Arthur Denny's grandmother, who was Martha Lynne's aunt; which is not to say that the Lynnes or the Forests were sympathetic to Crowmell, as both Martha Lynne's mother and

Elizabeth Forest had been ladies-in-waiting to Queen Elizabeth; and Stamford, the majestic home of Burghley, the Queen's chief minister, was quite near to the Lynne and the Forest homes. Capt. Hassett, a very acquisitive man by all appearances, hardly needed these Cromwellian connections; but they probably played a part in preserving the Denny estate for Sir Arthur Denny. Both Mary Hickson and Jeremiah King refer to a distant relationship between Forest and Cromwell. We also learn that the Wallers, ancestors of Sir Hardress Waller (the Limerick settler, who seems to have helped General Edmund Ludlow take Ross Castle), were old friends of the Dennys since the heyday of Margaret Edgcumbe. Waller and Ludlow signed the death warrant of Charles I; another signatory was a distant cousin of the Dennys, Sir George Fleetwood, one of Cromwell's generals, who was descended from a niece of the first Denny settler in Tralee.[68] Some years after the young Dennys returned from Bishop's Stortford, Arthur's sister, Elizabeth (the child at whose baptism Martha Lynne was present before the civil war), married a son of Capt. Hassett and Martha Lynne. Another John, he was *Cornet* John Blennerhassett. It was 1654, and for better or worse the destinies of the neighbouring families were now linked inextricably.

Southwick Hall, Northamptonshire

The young Dennys returned to a very changed environment. When Lord Muskerry surrendered Ross Castle, the surrender articles permitted the passage of thousands of Irish swordsmen to the continent to serve in the armies of the Catholic monarchies. Of the poorer people, we will never know the numbers of men, women and children transported to the barren lands of Connaught and Clare across the Shannon, or to the Caribbean islands, or the names of the priests who accompanied them. The clergy were excluded from the surrender articles, which "extend not to the exemption … nor to give p'tection to priests and Jesuites, or others in Popish Orders";[69] the Ross signatories included Frederick Mullins, John Nelson, Hardress Waller, Andrew Elliott, Francis Goold.

During the summer of 1652, when Ludlow took the surrender of Ross Castle and burned the Franciscan friary at Muckross, the Cromwellians occupied Tralee and destroyed Holy Cross. In the following year the Prior of Holy Cross, Thaddeus (Tadhg) Moriarty was hanged at Market Hill, Killarney, having been arrested at Kilclohane Wood while saying Mass. Executed there about the same time was Pierce Ferriter. Thaddeus Moriarty was born in Castledrum, and, following his priestly formation in Coimbra, Portugal, he taught at Bishop Rickard O'Connell's seminary in Tralee. There also, as Professor of Theology, was Fr Francis O'Sullivan, a native of Iveragh in the South of Kerry, who met his death when Cromwellian soldiers decapitated him on Scariff Island in the Kenmare River. Other religious escaped the martyr's fate because they served abroad in Europe. One of these was Fr Dominic O'Daly of Kilsarkan, whose ancestors were chroniclers to the earls of Desmond. Among his many writings, which included a History of the Geraldine earls of Desmond, is a record of the lives and martyrdoms of his priest colleagues in the Tralee region and beyond. Having studied with distinction at Alcalá de Henares, Spain, later ministering in Madrid, he founded a college for the Irish Dominican priests in Lisbon, and a college for the Dominican nuns in the same city. Modern scholarship has revealed his extraordinary career as a Portuguese diplomat after Portugal achieved independence from Spain under the Braganza dynasty in 1640.[70] The Braganza King of Portugal appointed O'Daly his first ambassador to Spain, and later O'Daly had a role in negotiating the marriage of Catherine of Braganza to Charles II of England.

In 1655, amidst continuing anarchy and desolation, a neighbour of the Blennerhassetts, the absentee Herbert, was permitted "to transport out of England and Wales 150 persons to plant his estate in Kerry, with their stocks and chattels", and to land them "at any port in Munster without custom or excise"; each settler was permitted to bring sixty fowling pieces "for their better security and encouragement".[71] Certain officers in Cromwell's army, including Collis, Bateman and Sandes, were given lands in lieu of cash. Hierome Sankey, their commanding officer, acquired lands in Ballymacelligott, Kilgobnet, Ballymacadam, Kilmaniheen and elsewhere, which he subsequently sold on. Capt. Hassett (Capt. "John Blennerhassett of Ballycarty") acquired lands from Sankey in Ballymacelligott in 1661 for a fee of £350 sterling, £250 of which was to be paid before 12th of November "at Strongbow's tomb in Christchurch, Dublin".[72] The Restoration settlement also confirmed Capt. John in his possession of those MacElligott lands given him by the Cromwellian settlement.

The return to the throne of Charles Stuart as Charles II in 1660 brought no satisfactory restoration to the dispossessed, in terms of either land or religious liberty, and the Cromwellian land settlement survived largely intact. In the Restoration Parliament of 1661 Capt. Hassett sat for the County, and his son Cornet John and the Cornet's brother-in-law Sir Arthur Denny sat for Tralee and the County respectively. It made a powerful statement about Blennerhassett political dominance in the Tralee region, and the likely permanence of the landed settlement.

Ballyseedy Castle (from th collection of the Knight of Glin)

The determination of the government to preserve penal restrictions against the Catholic religion compounded the disappointment of those hoping for a return of their estates; and though the Catholic-connected Ormond was restored to power in Dublin as the King's deputy, he was more than balanced by the puritanical Broghill who became President of Munster and was raised to the earldom of Orrery. The new residence of the Blennerhassetts belongs to this period: Ballyseedy. Cornet John Blennerhassett and his bride Elizabeth Denny were its first life residents, and it is given as their address in a deed of 1668, but it must represent a fitting recognition of the Cornet's parents, Capt. Hassett and the prestigious Martha Lynne's.[73] Sir Arthur Denny could boast nothing to compare with it. His Tralee Castle lay in ruins when he returned from Bishop's Stortford about 1650; then, as the price for being one of the *'49 officers* (those who had remained Royalist after King Charles's execution), part of his estate was given to Rowland Bateman, one of Cromwell's officers.

If the Blennerhassetts were scheming to inveigle the Tralee burgesses away from the Denny family at this early period, Sir Arthur's own marriage brought him some important political leverage. In 1651 he had married Lady Ellen Barry of Castlelyons, the daughter of Alice Boyle, daughter of Richard the Great Earl of Cork whose will of 1642 settled £1000 on his Barry granddaughter at her marriage.[74] Lady Ellen's uncle was Broghill, Cromwell's commander in Munster, who hanged the Catholic Bishop of Ross, Boetius MacEgan, outside Macroom in 1650, the year before the marriage. Sir Arthur and Lady Ellen Barry "beganne to keep howse in the greate Castle of Traly upon Thursday, Nov. … 1653", according to the Denny Family *Diary*. During the civil wars, Lady Ellen's father, the first Earl of Barrymore, died, apparently of wounds received at the battle of Liscarrol fighting for the English, while her mother's and Broghill's brother, Lord Kinalmeaky (Lewis Boyle), was killed in the same battle. Now, during the Restoration, Broghill (with the new title of Earl of Orrery), became Munster President. Through Ellen, therefore, Sir Arthur Denny became linked to a powerful family network in the Pale around Dublin, including Loftus, Jones and FitzGerald (Earl of Kildare), husbands of the Great Earl's other daughters, the sisters of Alice, Orrery and Kinalmeaky.

David Barry, 1st Earl Barrymore (seats Buttevant and Castlelyons).
Image supplied by Christie's

As the policies of Lord Orrery prevailed over those of the milder Ormond, Catholics were excluded from the government of the towns, and the South Munster towns were fortified during the invasion fears in 1663 and 1666. *Head money* continued to be offered for priests, especially those of the regular orders like Franciscans and Dominicans. From the Council Chamber, Dublin, Ormond issued a proclamation, dated 16 October 1678, announcing the renewal of expulsion orders of 27 October 1673 and 27 April 1674, requiring "All titular Popish Archbishops, bishops, vicars general, abbots, and all others exercising ecclesiastical jurisdiction … to depart out of His Majesty's Kingdom of Ireland"; also "all convents, seminaries, friaries, nunneries and Popish schools in this kingdom should be forthwith dissolved and suppressed".[75]

Sir Arthur Denny and Lady Ellen Barry died in 1673, to be followed in 1676 by that survivor from the earlier generation, Capt. Hassett. Of the fascinating Martha Lynne, whether she remained in Tralee or when she died, the available records are silent. Cornet John Blennerhassett, her and the Capt.'s son, fell ill and died in 1677.

5. JACOBITE PARLIAMENT OF 1689: ATTAINDER OF BLENNERHASSETT

The Denny heir was Colonel Edward Denny (b. 1652) who, in 1673, married Mary Maynard from Curryglass, a place situated near the Bride River in East Cork. This couple would preside at Tralee Castle in the years of turbulence generated by the King's brother and heir to the throne, the Catholic James, and James's secret arrangements with the King of France. In the 1670s, Colonel Edward's cousin Orrery was writing letters to Colonel Edward to warn of invasion.[76] Orrery was less than completely confident of Denny's capacity to protect Kerry, confiding that Denny and his father had converted Tralee Castle into "a convenient country gentleman's house".[77] The Castle was not the only problem: unlike Orrery, Colonel Edward exhibited the old loyalty of his family to the legitimate succession, which translated into a kind of lukewarm support for the hapless James. But such support would not save him from the Irish, and in 1691, at the latter end of the Williamite/Jacobite war, Tralee would be burnt by the Jacobites. Let us return to the course of events.

James succeeded his brother in 1685, and as king continued his dealings with King Louis. He promoted Richard Talbot of Malahide to the lord lieutenancy, and Talbot pursued a policy of depriving Protestant officers of their commissions in the Irish army and attacking the charters of the Irish corporations. Talbot received valuable assistance from Dingle man Sir Stephen Rice, James's Chief Baron of the (Irish) Exchequer. James fled his realm in 1688 and found refuge in France. His subjects deemed that he had abdicated the throne, so they brought in his son-in-law, William, Prince of Orange, to replace him as king. But James decided to fight for his throne, and he landed at Kinsale from Brest in March 1689, before making his way in stages to Dublin. In May, a French fleet under Admiral Chateaurenault attempted to land at Bantry. Weather was unfavourable, and when Admiral Herbert appeared, a sea battle commenced near Whiddy Island. Chateaurenault withdrew and returned to France.

Tralee Castle,
Water colour 1824, painted for Sir Edward Denny by his friend Sarah J. Harnett. "Quite a modern three-storied mansion, with 5 big windows, all in a row, attached to an older building which looked a blank wall." (Miss Rowan, "Some Old Tralee Notes", in *Kerry Archaeologicl Magazine* 1916, reproduced in *J.K.A.H.S.*, 1997, pp. 87, 89.)
"The (Castle) Court consisted of a green oval, with a carriage drive round going to the front of the then Castle, which was entered by a wide flight of stone steps." (*Kerry Evening Post*, 23 November 1895)

As the fleet departed, the Jacobite Parliament met in Dublin. All the leading supporters of William were attainted (sentenced to death or exile, and forfeiture of estates): not only had they abandoned their king and fled the country, but they had assisted "a most horrid Invasion … by your unnatural Enemy the Prince of Orange".[78] John Blennerhassett of Ballyseedy (son of Cornet John and his wife, Elizabeth Denny) and his cousin from Killorglin, "Black Jack" Blennerhassett, were attainted, along with the Batemans of Tralee, and Charles Petty (whose family would become the earls of Shelburne). "Black Jack" is the most interesting of the captives. Having been held in Galway by the Jacobites, then attainted, he survived to write the Blennerhassett genealogy. John Blennerhassett of Ballyseedy had a less distinguished war: he cut a deal with MacCarthy, one of the rebel leaders, leased him some land, and disappeared from Tralee while the war lasted. He may have had Jacobite sympathies (his wife was a Crosbie) and when he died, poet Aogán Ó Rathaille eulogised him, we think having once received a bed for the night.

King William and Queen Mary, from Cox's *Hibernia Anglicana*

Roger MacElligott of Ballymacelligott, an MP in the Jacobite Parliament for Ardfert, was no friend of the Blennerhassetts, MacElligott land having been granted to Capt. Hassett. Roger was a military man, somewhat hotheaded if we are to believe the account of his conduct at Portsmouth, where he commanded a company of soldiers during the war and shot up the church.

The tables were turned on the Jacobites and their Parliament (whose existence is expunged from the official record) by the victories of the William on the battlefield. The greatest of these was the Boyne. James fled the Boyne and never stopped until he reached Duncannon Fort in South Wexford. There, Sir Patrick Trant of Dingle (very probably a cousin of Sir Stephen Rice) received James on board his ship and took him to France. Later, the forces of William took Limerick, the siege of which was the final important action involving the armies of the two kings. Tralee was burned as the siege of Limerick dragged on. Lady Denny (Mary Maynard) had been assured that if the Castle were surrendered the town would be spared – but the promise was reneged upon. It is possible that the Jacobites intended to save the town and that Colonel Denny's absence made them change their minds. The deed is recorded in the Denny Bible:

> "The second of September 1691 the Mansion House, the Castell of Tralee, the seat of that worthy and loyal gentleman Edward Denny, Esq., was burnd by Coll. Ruth, by order of Sir James Cotter, Knight, who was the Governor of this County Kerry, after he had received a good sum from Madam Denny to save it, and engaged his hand and faith to the performance, butt not like a gentleman broke his engagement."

William had successfully defended the throne against James. Coningsby and Porter, the two Irish lord justices, arrived at Limerick in October 1691 after that city's surrender, and there they signed the Treaty of Limerick on behalf of the Williamites. Coningsby's daughter will shortly enter the Tralee story.

[51] Tralee's Charter is reproduced as an appendix in Mary F. Cusack, *A History of the Kingdom of Kerry*, 1895.

[52] *Cal. S.P ., Carew 1603-24*, p. 289; King James, Whitehall, to the recusant lords of Ireland, 20 April 1614.

[53] Treadwell.

[54] *Cal. S. P Ireland, James I, 1606-1608*, p.256, year 1607: Sir Arthur Chichester, Lord Deputy of Ireland, dated 26 August 1607, forwarded to the Chief Justice and Chief Baron.

[55] Ibid., p.257.

[56] Denny Family *Diary*, transcribed by Henry L.L. Denny, in *Memorials of the Dead*, vol. 7; the same material was published by Rev. Sir H.L.L. Denny in the *Journal of The County Kerry Society*.

[57] Charles Smith, *Antient and Present State of The County of Kerry*, Rev. H. L.L. Denny, *Memorials of the Dead*; *Reports from the Commissioners on the Municipal Corporations in Ireland 1835, Borough of Tralee*.

[58] Maurice G. McElligott, "Some Kerry Wild Geese", in *The Irish Genealogist*, vol. 2, no. 8, October 1950, pp. 250-254, p.251. The wife of the famous English divine Dr Thomas Fuller was Mary, daughter of Lord Baltinglass and sister of (Ruth Roper) Lady Denny of Tralee Castle.

[59] Mary Hickson, "The Knights of St John in Kerry and Limerick", in *J.H.A.A.I.*, vol. 9, 1889, pp. 184-191.

[60] Fr Myles Nolan, OP, "Tralee Dominicans, Survival and Service", in McConville, Seamus, *The Dominicans of Tralee*, 1987, p.9.

[61] Aidan Clarke, *The Old English in Ireland*, 1625-42, 2000, Appendix III, p. 257.

[62] Sloane Ms. no. 10081 (anon.), in Herbert Webb Gillman, "The Rise and Progress in Munster of the Rebellion, 1642", *J.C.H.A.S.*, November 1895, pp. 529-542, p. 535.

[63] Richard Butler, 3rd Viscount Mountgarret led the Confederate Irish. He was accompanied by a number of his Butler kinsmen from Kilkenny, joined by Roche, and MacDonogh, chief of Duhallow.

[64] Jeremiah King, *History of Kerry, or History of the Parishes in the County*, 1908-14, p. 249.

[65] St. John D. Seymour, B. D., *Adventures and Experiences of a XVIIth Century Clergyman, edited from the Original Manuscript*, Dublin 1909.

[66] *The Inchiquin Manuscripts*, Inchiquin testimonial for David Crosbie, 6 July 1647. Crosbie, of Ardfert, paid a high price for his sacrifice; Inchiquin tells us that Crosbie "hath lost an estate of about £800 per annum ... detained from him by the said rebels and ... his suffering hath been great in the service of the Parliament ".

[67] King, *History of Kerry*, p. 249.

[68] *The Complete Peerage*, Fleetwood; Hickson, *Kerry Evening Post*, 9 December 1893; the Waller friendship did "yeoman's service" to the Dennys, according to Mary Hickson.

[69] *Archivium Hibernicum*, 1918-21, "The Commonwealth Records", pp. 20-66: Articles at Ross (Castle) with ye Lo: Muskerry.

[70] Margaret MacCurtain, "An Irish Agent of the Counter-Reformation, Dominic O'Daly", in *Irish Historical Studies*, September 1967.

[71] W. J. Smith, *Herbert Correspondence*, University of Wales, 1963, 1968 edn., pp. 142.

[72] Transcribed deed in a bound volume entitled the *Blennerhassett Pedigree* in the possession of the Knight of Glin.

[73] *Blennerhassett Pedigree*: the marriage settlement is dated 1654; the Dennys agreed £500 stg. "for the preferment and portion" of the bride-to-be, Elizabeth. Martha Lynne, through her father George Lynne, and back through the Nevilles and Throckmortons, linked the Blennerhassetts, Ventrys, Dennys and many other Kerry families to the Plantagenets: Joseph Foster, *The Royal Lineage of Our Noble and Gentle Families*, vol. 2, 1887, Judge de Moleyns, Q.C.; James Franklin Fuller wrote: "in my county of Kerry, Plantagenet blood is so common that we don't think it worth while to be 'stuck up' about it." (James F. Fuller, *Omniana, The Autobiography of an Irish Octogenarian*, London 1916, p.281.)

[74] Dorothea Townshend, *The Life and Letters of the Great Earl of Cork*, London 1904, p.488. It was a case of two weddings: Lady Ellen's sister married Denny's brother, and the Great Earl settled a similary legacy on her.

[75] *H.M.C.* Ormond, vol.2, p. 350.

[76] *H.M.C.* Ormond, Earl of Orrery, Castlemartyr, to Edward Denny, 28 January 1678.

[77] King, *History of Kerry*, p. 245.

[78] William King, *The State of the Protestants of Ireland Under the Late King James's Government*, London 1691.

FOUR
OLIGARCHY

1. Reign of William and Mary (1688-1702): the Penal Laws

The Treaty of Limerick, following the victory of William at the Boyne and the fall of Limerick, established the narrow and exclusive Protestant nation of the eighteenth century. As the defeated military prepared to swell the ranks of the Irish Brigade in Europe (their brothers and cousins enrolling in the continental colleges to train for the priesthood), the Irish Parliament prepared to introduce further penal legislation for what would become the century of the Penal Laws.

New anti-tory (outlaw) legislation had southern coastal counties like Kerry very much in mind. Invasion was an ever-present danger, and the English navy under Sir George Rooke destroyed the French at La Hogue in 1692. French agents were everywhere and the Kerry coastline offered many attractive coves and inlets for the trade in contraband.

The Dominicans, who had existed in scattered communities since Cromwellian times, faced a renewed wave of persecution: the *Banishment of Religious* Act of 1697 came into force in May 1698. The Provincial Definitory of the Franciscans decided to obey the Act in principle: goods would be given into safe keeping, and novices sent to the continent, while permission would be sought for the old and infirm friars to remain in Ireland.[79] The persecution of their comrades the diocesan priests is recorded by Canon Burke in his book *The Irish Priests in Penal Times*:

> "Donagh McCarthy, parish priest of Tralee in the Co. of Kerry is Dean of Ardfert and took his tryall as soe, and since the death of Dr. Daly who dyed in (16)99 in Corke Jayle he makes use of the power of Jurisdiction of Aghadar in the Co. of Kerry".[80]

As the Williamite Parliament met in 1692, the Blennerhassetts had cause to believe that they rather than the Dennys should inherit the governance of Tralee. Blennerhassett commitment to the Williamite campaign was never in doubt, and leading family members had been attainted, while Col. Edward Denny had escaped attainder and left the defense of Tralee to Mary Maynard. However, a new family now advanced to prominence: Thomas FitzMaurice, twenty-first Lord Kerry (of Lixnaw) and erstwhile Jacobite, married Anne Petty in 1692, and in the same year FitzMaurice and Denny were returned to Parliament for the County. FitzMaurice had been in France with King James, but with James's defeat in Ireland he considered it prudent to make his peace with the Protestant state – which he did with his marriage to the Cromwellian Petty. The extraordinary change in the fortunes of the FitzMaurices did not end there. Although John Blennerhassett of Ballyseedy (son of Cornet John) was returned to Parliament for Tralee, the other MP for Tralee was James Waller, a son of the regicide Sir Hardress Waller; and James Waller's sister Elizabeth was Anne Petty's mother.[81].

2. REIGN OF ANNE (1702-1714) AND OF GEORGE I (1714-1727): THE TRALEE OF LETITIA CONINGSBY

Letitia Coningsby was a spectacular match for the Denny heir, another Edward. She was the daughter of a leading figure of the Williamite Revolution, though Letitia's husband, Edward, seems too young to have played a part in that conflict. Her arrival is recorded in the Denny Bible.

"1700 The 3d of October came to Tralee the … Madam Liticia Denny the daughter of the Right Honble Thomas Lord Coningsbee she made hir entry with divers gentillmen of qualety and aboute 200 horse of the tennaunts and shee and hir husbund received with much joye in the castill of Tralee by the father Coll: Edward Denny and the mother Madam Denny and by all the noble relations."

Letitia's father was Sir Thomas Coningsby, of Hampton Court in Herefordshire. The night before the Battle of the Boyne, William of Orange was wounded when on recognisance; an eye witness recorded how Coningsby "seeing his Majesty struck, rid up and put his handkerchief upon the place".[82] Such devotion brings its reward and Coningsby occupied positions at the very top of the Irish and English governments during the reign of William and Mary, and remained a figure of exceptional influence in the two reigns that followed. His mother was a Loftus of Rathfarnham, the same family with which Lady Ellen Barry (a previous Denny wife) was connected through the marriage of one of her Boyle aunts. Coningsby had already given a daughter to the region in the person of Letitia's sister, Meliora, who had married Sir Thomas Southwell, first Baron Southwell of Castlematrix in Limerick; he had been in the Williamite army, was captured in Galway, then attainted by the Jacobite Parliament, and in the end pardoned.[83]

Queen Anne's accession, two years after Letitia's arrival in Tralee, coincided with the renewal of war with France, the War of the Spanish Succession, which brought the inevitable threat of invasion and a Jacobite revival. Catholic priests were compelled to register under the Act of 1703 (in the following year thirty-six priests from County Kerry did so at the quarter sessions),[84] and the 1704 Popery Act introduced a range of disabilities including the subdivision of Catholic estates on inheritance. The Oath taken by the burgess men on election to the Denny corporation of Tralee was modelled on the Act of 1691, which excluded Catholics from government office, the legal profession and commissions in the army and navy. The Oath condemned Transubstantiation, also "the invocation or adoration of the Virgin Mary or any other Saint and the Sacrifice of the Mass", and the dispensing power of the Pope.[85] Anne's succession was secured by the string of victories under the Duke of Marlborough (John Churchill), notably Blenheim. When the Old Pretender attempted an invasion of Scotland in 1708, Lord Kenmare and MacCarthy Mór and some others were confined in Tralee, but they were soon released, possibly through the intervention of Blennerhassett.

Theodosia Bligh,
wife of William Crosbie, 1st Earl of Glandore. The Crosbies of Ardfert were allies
of the Dennys who were intermarried with the FitzMaurices of Lixnaw, lords Kerry.

The Whigs were supplanted in 1710 by a Tory administration. Queen Anne herself, a daughter of James II, was known to have Tory sympathies, and Jonathan Swift wrote propaganda for her new government. Swift had a couple of Kerry friends in Lord Kerry (Thomas FitzMaurice) and his wife Anne (Petty), who must have spent many days at her brother's mansion in Dublin, on the site of the present Shelburne Hotel. Then their daughter, Arabella FitzMaurice, married the heir of Edward and Letitia, Colonel Arthur Denny, a move which must have brought the influence of the Lixnaw family into Tralee Castle itself and further distanced the Blennerhassetts of Ballyseedy from the seat of power in Tralee. In fact, the Blennerhassetts were now encircled: Arabella's sister was the wife of Sir Maurice Crosbie, and Sir Maurice's sister had married the Knight of Kerry in 1703. The Knight controlled the borough of Dingle. The Crosbie borough, Ardfert, had returned two leading Jacobites to King

James's Parliament: Roger MacElligott and Cornelius MacGillicuddy. In the century ahead, Ardfert would never return a Blennerhassett.

Letitia's husband Edward Denny died in 1728, after which Letitia is said to have returned to Hampton Court, her father's home. She died about 1749, according to the Denny Family Diary.[86] Tradition credits her with having laid out the Bowling Green at the back of Tralee Castle, which she modelled on that at Hampton Court. Their son, Colonel Arthur Denny, succeeded.

3. GEORGE II (1727-1760): THE GREAT COLONEL JOHN BLENNERHASSETT COVETS THE BOROUGH OF TRALEE

For much of the long reign of George II the management of government business in Ireland was in the hands of the parliamentary managers, or *undertakers*, principally Speaker Henry Boyle (later Earl of Shannon). Boyle was a grandson of Lord Orrery, and he controlled that constellation of parliamentary boroughs in South Munster inherited from Orrery's father, the Great Earl of Cork (whose granddaughter, Lady Ellen Barry, had married an earlier Arthur Denny at the end of the Cromwell wars).

Colonel Arthur Denny became an MP for the County in the first Parliament of George II; however, Denny dominance was eclipsed, and the control of their corporation usurped, by the considerable figure of the *Great Colonel* John Blennerhassett of Ballyseedy, son and namesake of the Blennerhassett eulogised by poet Aogán Ó Rathaille. Colonel John coveted the borough of Tralee. In his heyday, the Great Colonel aspired to the degree of political power to which he believed his inheritance and his extensive family network entitled him. Descended from both Martha Lynne and Ruth Roper, he was married (settlement 1713) to Jane, daughter of Sir Edward Denny and Mary Maynard; and he was able to harness the impressive numbers of his Killorglin cousins, who had inherited the estate of Elizabethan planter Jenkin Conway, as well as his Blennerhassett marriage connections with Rowan and Mullins, from Castlegregory and Burnham respectively on the Dingle Peninsula, and Rowan, Wren, Stoughton and Spring. Now in 1727, at the accession of George II, having represented the County since the reign of Anne, Colonel John transferred himself into one of the Tralee seats; and, together with Colonel Arthur Denny and Sir Maurice Crosbie (of Ardfert), the two County MPs, he formed the *Agreement Tripartite*, or *Family Compact*, to parcel out the County and Borough seats in future elections. The arrangement lasted for many years. In Parliament the *Compact* usually voted with Speaker Boyle as part of Boyle's *Munster Squadron*, however it did not share Boyle's narrow definition of Protestant patriotism: the lawlessness of Kerry and its distance from the centre of power meant that the participants in the *Compact* were inclined to switch support to other sources of patronage, which at some future date might include the Crown's representative. All shades of opinion in Dublin believed Kerry politicians were beneficiaries of smuggling, a view bolstered by the enquiry that followed the Danish Silver Robbery at Ballyheigue in 1730 which revealed the worrying extent of collusion between the thieves and the forces of law-and-order.

The untimely death of Colonel Arthur Denny in 1742, following on the death of his father-in-law Thomas FitzMaurice, first Earl of Kerry, in the previous year, tempted the Great Colonel Blennerhassett to jettison the Family Compact. Family turmoil, to some degree attributable to the violent character of the Earl of Kerry, weakened the Lixnaws' participation in politics from as early as the 1730s, long before the agriculturalist Arthur Young witnessed the abandoned condition of Old Court forty years later. At first the Great Colonel was reduced to the role of bystander when Colonel Arthur Denny's seat in the County was filled by Arthur's brother-in-law John FitzMaurice. But then an opportunity arose for the Great Colonel to strike at the Dennys in Tralee itself. This was a vacancy created in 1743 when the Great Colonel's colleague MP for the town, Arthur Blennerhassett of Riddlestown, Rathkeale (who despite his name was a Denny nominee), was appointed a judge. The Ballyseedy Blennerhassetts now tabled the nomination of the Great Colonel's son, another Arthur Blennerhassett, and the Great Colonel set about suborning the Denny burgesses to secure his son's election. The Denny camp countered by nominating another Limerick man, one of their cousins, the young Thomas Southwell, third Baron Southwell and future first Viscount. At the election in late October, Southwell was deemed to have won the seat, but Arthur, the Great Colonel's son, petitioned Parliament, citing the "utmost partiality" on the part of the Provost, who presided at the return, for having admitted a number of non-legitimate voters favourable to Southwell, at the same time disenfranchising some burgesses who intended voting for the petitioner. The petitioner claimed to have still won the poll, only to have his election set aside by the Provost. The petition was successful: the disenfranchised burgesses were reinstated; Southwell, who had already taken his seat in Parliament, was removed, and Arthur Blennerhassett put in his place.[87] Meanwhile, the fortunes of the FitzMaurices continued to decline: Thomas, the first Earl of Kerry, who died in 1741, was followed quickly to the grave by his son, the second Earl, whose children were brought to Dublin to be raised as wards of court by Lord Chancellor Jocelyn. The first Earl's second son, John FitzMaurice, vacated the County to succeed to the Shelburne estates, and his seat was taken by John, first son and heir of the Great Colonel; this "John Blennerhassett the younger" and his more able brother, Arthur who petitioned against Southwell, remained MPs for the rest of the reign of George II, for the County and Tralee respectively.

Judge Arthur Blennerhassett (of Riddlestown House, near Rathkeale), MP Tralee.
In the final quarter of the century Tralee and Ardfert returned many eminent law men to the
old Irish Parliament, including John Toler (later Lord Norbury), William Fletcher,
Arthur Moore, Henry Kemmis (all Tralee); Arthur Wolfe, Robert Day and John Scott (all Ardfert).

4. GOVERNMENT AND GOVERNANCE IN THE ERA OF SIR THOMAS DENNY

The Blennerhassetts dominance in the elections – father and son sitting for Tralee, and another son sitting for the County – consigned the Dennys to what appears a reduced political role, that of the day-to-day governance of Tralee and the Denny estate. The Denny vote remained considerable in the County where, according to the *Pocket Rental* of Sir Thomas, dated 1750, "Sir Thomas Denny hath on his estate one hundred and seventy seven substantial freeholders of his own and his family's making to elect representatives to serve in Parliament for the County of Kerry, and there are not in the whole County besides above two hundred and twenty". Sir Thomas was successor to his brother, Colonel Arthur, and in 1743 Sir Thomas wrote a will as the Blennerhassett petition was being entertained in Parliament. While he wrote it, he seemed to anticipate the removal of Southwell from Parliament: he denounced the burgesses removed by his family and restored by Parliament, then instructed the guardians of his children to "keep a watchful eye on the Family of the Blennerhassetts to prevent their undermining my said children in their interest in the Burough of Traly" (the Blennerhassetts having) "made attacks on my Life, Estate and Fortune".[88] Sir Thomas probably moved into Tralee Castle on Colonel Arthur's death, yet even here the Great Colonel John had a foothold: Sir Thomas's wife, the new Lady Denny (m. 1740), was the Great Colonel's daughter, Agnes Blennerhassett, who was about fifteen years younger than her husband. A Blennerhassett presence at the baptisms of the couple's children is in doubt, at the first of which (1741/2) the sponsors are Sir Thomas's cousin Lord Southwell, Sir Arthur's widow Arabella, and Arabella's brother, the second Earl of Kerry.[89]

Sir Thomas Denny had plenty to occupy him in and around Tralee. His family held the advowsons of a number of parishes, which included the right to appoint the church minister: Tralee itself, Ballinahaglish (Churchill), Clogherbrien, Annagh, and Kilgobbin (Camp). He served as Deputy Governor of Kerry and colonel of an independent regiment of dragoons arrayed in 1745 as part of the militia to confront a possible landing by the Young Pretender during the War of the Austrian Succession.[90] The French success at Fontenoy that year, with the Irish Brigade performing to distinction, must have rekindled Protestant fears around Tralee. Britain gave diplomatic assurances to her ally Austria that she would soft-pedal the implementation of the penal laws, yet there was no official role for Catholics in Sir Thomas's militia, and Catholics would not win the right to bear arms until the legislation of 1793. When the Pretender landed in Scotland there was no sympathetic rebellion in Ireland, and Catholic bishops urged their people to remain loyal to King George. "Bonnie Prince Charlie" was finally defeated at Culloden in 1746 and the threat of a Jacobite restoration passed. Some believe that the famine of 1741 – little known today but quite widespread at the time – dampened any intentions to support the Pretender; others stress the role of Lord Chesterfield (Stanhope), who was Irish Lord Lieutenant during *the '45*, as a calming influence on Protestant fears. The Peace of Aix-la-Chapelle in 1748 marked the end of the war.

Celebrations in Dublin (1748) on hearing the Aix-la-Chapelle Peace Conference
(courtesy of the National Library of Ireland)

Denny probably served on the Grand Jury, the body charged with the local government of the County. The Grand Jury heard presentments at the time of the Assizes for the construction of roads and bridges and for public health, and these were ratified by the judges. In municipal politics, Tralee's parish Vestry took much of the weight of responsibility for the day to day running of the town, including tasks such as town paving and flagging; the townspeople paid the vestry cess levied for this purpose. The poor of both town and countryside paid hearth money, a tax dating from the time of Charles II the assessment for which was based on the number of fireplaces in a dwelling. Towards the end of the century a window tax was added. A subset of the Grand Jury, twelve in number, was empanelled as the Petit Jury to try cases at the Assizes. Kerry's twice-yearly Assizes were held in the same block as the old County Jail, the building on our right as we enter the Square from the Mall, the Jail occupying the downstairs level. The Assembly Room would later occupy the level upstairs: "The block of buildings facing the Mall was the Assembly Room, where the beauty and fashion of Kerry held their dances ... In this same block was the Court House, also the Jail, of that day."[91] Justices of the peace (magistrates) held quarter-sessions in the smaller towns, and offenders were detained in bridewells, to be brought later to the County Jail if convicted. Often the justices were clergymen, Hickson, Graves, Day, Herbert, Hewson, the "tithe-eating tribe of parson-justices" of whom William Cobbett wrote.

Ireland experienced an economic boom during Thomas Denny's time, the government issuing hundreds of licenses for fairs and markets throughout the country. But Tithe paid to the parson, usually collected by a tithe farmer or his tithe proctor, remained the scourge of the rural poor. Butter exports soared, and the Butter Road was filled with ponies drawing their distinctive butter firkins on the journey to the Cork butter exchange, there to supply the needs of Britain's wars and her expanding Empire. Around Tralee and into the Dingle Peninsula the evidence of flax and the linen industry was everywhere, and the linen board in Dublin took advertising space in the press to advertise premiums for the different categories of the finished product. In old deeds we often find mention of bleach greens and *scutch* (scotch) mills. A Tralee lease preserved in our National Archives, bearing the date 1 November 1798, has "(the) tenement called the Nursery Tenement ...dwelling house formerly held by Philip Grady linen weaver ... bounded on the east with the Rock tenement ...and the west by Chappel lane leading to the Quarry ...".[92] Most cottages had a spinning wheel. The Charter school at Castleisland taught linen manufacture as part of the curriculum.

About the middle of the century the Great Colonel John Blennerhassett introduced a number of Palatine families from the Southwell estate near Rathkeale. They were the descendants of those driven out of their homes in the German Palatinate in 1709 in the war waged by King Louis XIV of France. Agriculturist Arthur Young recorded these Palatines when he visited the Great Colonel in the 1770s.

Colonel Arthur Denny's widow, Lady Arabella (*née* FitzMaurice), was settled in Dublin by the time the Austrian Succession War began, having departed Tralee after Arthur's death. She became associated with the Dublin Foundling Hospital about 1750, and became the only lady member of the Phisico Historical Society, the society which sent Charles Smith to write histories of Waterford, Cork and Kerry. (Smith's Kerry *History* was published 1756.) She lived in Dublin for about forty years, first in Dorset St, then in Blackrock where John Wesley visited her during one of his many visits to Ireland. In 1766 or 1767 she founded the Magdalen Asylum in Lower Leeson Street, Dublin, which "rescued hundreds of unfortunate poor girls from misery and destruction, and by her noble and humane institution of the Irish Magdalen, fed them, clothed them, and put them in the fair road of future salvation" (*Freeman's Journal*, 15 January 1789).[93]

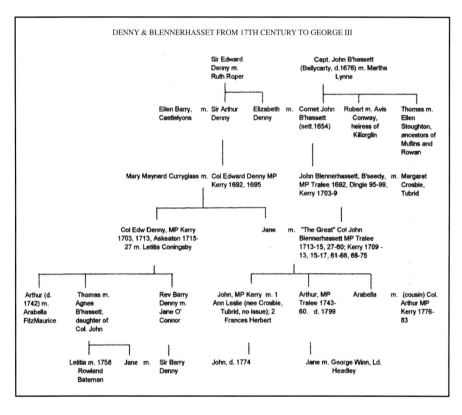

The Great Colonel and his sons were in Parliament for the money surplus controversy with the government at the end of 1753 when some of the old Family Compact supported Boyle's attempt to withhold control of the budget surplus from the grasp of the government. After the controversy ended with the government defeat, supporters of the Blennerhassetts and Sir Maurice Crosbie of Ardfert (the other MP for the County) prepared an address of congratulation: these "principal gentlemen and freeholders of the said county" met in Tralee on 6 April 1754 to honour their hero MPs, for "your truly wise and patriotic conduct".[94] A counter address was prepared by the government camp, which included Sir Thomas Denny, who, it is worth remembering, was distantly related through the Boyles to two of the Dukes of Devonshires (Cavendish), holders of the viceroyalty in the 1730s and again in the 1740s.

Sir Thomas and Agnes hosted the historian Charles Smith and travel writer and classicist Richard Pococke, the future Bishop of Ossory. Smith's map shows one branch of the Big River no longer flowing down the route of what is now Denny Street. He saw no remains of the Dominican Abbey, though he heard that it used to have a very fair steeple. Pococke had travelled in the Middle East and throughout Western Europe. In August 1758, he found Tralee "a poor irregular town". Sir Thomas Denny was living in the Castle, there was "a plain market house in the Square, and a neat new built Church on one side of the town". Hardly anything survived of Holy Cross, "except one near arch'd building, which probably was the chapel for the burial of the Desmond family, for near it are found pieces of a fine old monument it may be of that family."[95] Pococke's "neat new built Church" seems to date the reconstruction of St John's (on the present Ashe Street) to the middle of the century. De Burgo, author of *Hibernia Dominicana*, confirmed the ruin of Holy Cross: "Although the church and priory have been completely leveled, still on the site, or in streets nearby, there are still to be seen several burial stones ..."

Market House.
The Market House, or "Pedlars Change", stood on the north side of the Square. It housed the old County Jail and the twice-yearly Assize Court for County Kerry. Later the Assizes were held in another building, and the vacated Court Room was turned into an Assembly Room, where balls and concerts, often attended by the Kerry Militia, were in full swing during the Napoleonic war.

There were fresh fears of a Brest invasion fleet in 1755. Dublin heard that French officers had landed in Munster. Then there was full-blown war between England and France from 1756: the Seven Year War. King George III ascended the throne in 1760, and Sir Thomas died in the following year. He was succeeded by his nephew, the future Sir Barry Denny. During the war

Lady Arabella Denny's nephew, the Shelburne heir, briefly represented the County of Kerry (the *Journal* of the House of Commons refers to him as "William Petty, commonly called Lord Viscount FitzMaurice"); then he inherited the title, resigned from the army and moved into government as President of the Board of Trade, coming under the influence of the great war minister William Pitt. Later in the century, Barry Denny would be given a baronetage, probably through Shelburne's influence, whose very high estimate of his aunt is clear from Shelburne's autobiography.

William Petty, Earl of Shelburne, 1st Marquess Lansdowne

LADY ARABELLA DENNY, PHILANTHROPIST

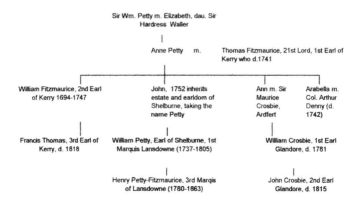

[79] Patrick Conlan OFM, *Franciscan Ireland* (Cork 1978), p.39.

[80] Report of Lord Rochester, taken from the Southwell Papers, Canon William Burke, *The Irish Priests in the Penal Times, 1660-1760.*

[81] Samuel Morris, of Ballybeggan, attainted by the Jacobite Parliament, occupied one of the Tralee seats from 1703 for twenty years. He seems to have been closely related to Southwell and Raymond, also attainted.

[82] G. Storey, *A True and Impartial History of the Kingdom of Ireland During the Two last Years* (London 1691), p. 75.

[83] Southwell later represented Co. Limerick in the Parliaments of William and Anne.

[84] Liam Chambers, "The Irish Colleges in 17th and 18th Century Paris: A Brief History", *The Kerry Magazine*, 2009, p.40.

[85] Reproduced in *K.E.P.* 20 June 1888; see transcription of 3 William and Mary c. 2 in Maureen Wall, "The Age of the Penal Laws" in T.W. Moody and F.X. Martin, *The Course of Irish History* (Cork 1967), p. 219.

[86] *Denny Family Diary*, transcribed by Sir H.L.L. Denny in *Memorials of the Dead*, vol. 7, p. 367.

[87] *H.C. Jn. (Ir.)*, vol. 7, 1739-46, pp. 357, 430, 463, 465, 484. Year 1743.

[88] Will of Sir Thomas Denny in the possession of Rev. Sir H.L.L. Denny, quoted by him in *County Kerry Society Annual Reports 1922-40*. The offending burgesses were Thomas Hilliard, Dr. William Collis and Edward Day.

[89] *Denny Family Diary*, in *Memorials of the Dead*, vol. 7.

[90] *Ibid.*, p. 367. For the continuing presence of Lord Kerry (Lixnaw) in the 1745 militia, see *A List of Officers in the Several Regiments and Independent Troops and Companies of Militia in Ireland, taken from the Books in the Secretaries' Offices, Dublin*, printed 1761.

[91] Annie Rowan in *K.E.P.*, 19 October 1895.

[92] N.A.I.,1025/3/12/8.

[93] *L.C.*, Saturday, 31 March 1792: Lady Denny's funeral reported as it passed through Limerick, including her hearse "drawn by six horses". The *Kerry Magazine* 1856 remembered a "most remarkable circumstance attending the funeral … the 'wailing of the twelve mourners' "; these were "twelve widows who each received two suits of black yearly and donations at festivals, from her ladyship, since the death of Colonel Arthur, her husband".

[94] The *Universal Advertiser*, 11 May 1754, in the *Kerry Evening Post*, 12 October 1892.

[95] *J.C.H.A.S.* 1959, Richard Pococke, *Tour of the South of Ireland*, 1758.

FIVE
REFORM

1. REIGN OF GEORGE III, ENLIGHTENED REFORM

The new King's coronation address promised governance for *all* communities, and this raised expectation among Ireland's majority. However, many were not persuaded that the Jacobite threat had disappeared. Prussia under King Frederick II was Pitt's ally in the war with France, and when Britain declared war on Spain (France's ally) in 1761, the mood among the Irish ruling class was hostile to change. Then the Whiteboy insurrection in Munster in the following year accentuated all the old fears of Catholic sedition. The Devonshire estate at Lismore suffered the effects of the insurrection, and, though Kerry appears to have escaped (if we are to believe contemporary witnesses), the Tralee oligarchy had a fresh argument to justify its exclusive constitution.

If Barry Denny had aspirations to reassert the Denny influence over the corporation when he moved into Tralee Castle on the death of his uncle Sir Thomas Denny in 1761 (Sir Thomas having no male heirs), they must have been short lived. Rowland Bateman of Oak Park and Barry Denny were married to daughters of Sir Thomas, and yet Bateman's return to Parliament for Tralee in that same year is more indicative of the enduring influence of Colonel John Blennerhassett, Sir Thomas's father-in-law, than of a break in the Blennerhassett monopoly of the Tralee representation; and Edward Herbert of Muckross, Colonel John's son-in-law, took the other Tralee seat. The father-and-son Ballyseedy presence in the Tralee elections was, however, at an end. Arthur Blennerhassett resided in Dublin and became more and more preoccupied with the task of bringing some order to the financial affairs of his father; thereafter he was bound for the life of an absentee in England. The Great Colonel himself represented the County constituency from 1761, and it was here that he ended a parliamentary career of over sixty years as Father of the House.[96]

The Dublin and provincial press had by now penetrated Kerry, helped initially by a regular letter post which began early in the century.[97] Sir Thomas Denny had placed notices to his tenantry in a Limerick newspaper, *The Munster Journal*, during the 1740s; it and the likes of *The Limerick Chronicle* were circulating in Kerry long before the founding of *The Kerry Evening Post* in 1774.[98] Such was the apparent abundance of newspapers by Barry Denny's time that we read of a distribution dispute; the story is printed in *The Cork Journal* of 28 May 1761, the Cork bookseller Phineas Bagnell included among the disputants. The press carried Britain's argument with her American colonists over taxation which began in the early 1760s, together with the fame of Benjamin Franklin, and Shelburne's return to government under Pitt in 1766. At this early stage all communities could identify with the complaints of the colonists, not least because America was considered a kind of rural paradise where the teachings of Rousseau could find practical expression far away from the bad governance of old Europe; the more youthful members of the leisured class experimented with *rustication* by building grottos and chalets in the midst of wild nature, others forsook their churches to join Masonic lodges, or hell-fire clubs like the one founded by the gentry of West Limerick.

The Irish Parliament produced new legislation in the fields of health and penal reform, thereby reflecting the thinking of such as Voltaire, who espoused American freedoms (he admired William Penn's colony at Pennsylvania) and penal reform in his native France. The construction of the County Infirmary in Tralee was provided for under the Act of 1765 and later opened at Strand Street. The Protestant bishop and the rector of the town were to be the local representatives on the Infirmary board. Kerry was specifically mentioned in the legislation. A later Act[99]recommended "John Murphy of the town of Tralee in the county of Kerry surgeon, (who) served several years on board his Majesty's fleet, and is from long experience and practice the fittest and most able in the said county to attend and take care of the infirmary and hospital, now erected or hereafter to be erected and established in the said town of Tralee and county aforesaid, pursuant to the said act". Yet some years later the Irish Parliament heard that the Kerry Infirmary was an old building with eight rooms, now in a "most wretched condition ... the very roof is tottering".[100]

Progress in penal reform drew its inspiration from campaigns in France. Lord Shelburne, consigned again with Pitt to the opposition benches as the war with the American colonists approached, travelled to France in the 1770s where he befriended the French penal reformer, the Abbé Morellet, who was influenced by the famous Milanese, Cesare Beccaria. Morellet knew Voltaire, and Voltaire had led a number of campaigns to expose cetain celebrated miscarriages of justice in France which he believed were the product of the unholy alliance of the Catholic Church and the Bourbon monarchy.[101] How Shelburne's experience may have influenced his Kerry admirers can only be a matter of speculation, but we know that the very energetic Chief Secretary Thomas Orde was a disciple of Shelburne and Pitt; and Orde, ably assisted by Robert Day among others, introduced the rural police into Kerry. That was in the decade of the Rightboys, to be considered shortly.

2. GRATTAN'S VOLUNTEERS, THE AMERICAN WAR OF INDEPENDENCE

For those who hoped that reform would bring the removal of the Penal Laws against Catholics, disappointment was in store. The power of the great borough magnates, who ran the Irish Parliament for so long, suffered a blow in the early 1770s when Viceroy Townshend pushed through his policy to augment the army, in doing so loosening the old stranglehold of Lord Shannon and his clique. But in 1773 the outlaw Art O'Leary was shot in West Cork while home on furlough from the Hungarian Hussars, and in the following year the gentry of Tralee (the Blennerhassett clan strongly represented) voted a resolution condemning the reappearance of Jacobites, who "have dared to drink Toasts and make use of expressions highly disrespectful to the illustrious House of Hanover".[102] The Catholics maintained their discipline, agreeing an oath of allegiance with the government, and one of the MPs for Tralee, Sir Boyle Roche, encouraged the government to consider recruiting Catholics for service in America.[103]

The Great Colonel John Blennerhassett finally passed away in May 1775.[104] He died at Oak Park, home of his Bateman granddaughter. There he wrote his will, and there also one of his daughters-in-law, Jane, wife of his second son Arthur, visited him from Bath in the year before his death:

"Our old father, at 82, is what you would style 'a jolly dog'; he is straight, teeth and sight good, hearing a little thick; is polite, cheerful, and even droll; sits to his bottle constantly till nine or ten o'clock, and never wishes to go to bed till one or two in the morning; vastly happy to see us, and mighty fond of his grand-daughters".[105]

Then tragedy stuck when the old man's principal heir (the son of his deceased first-born, John) died later in the year of Jane's visit. Jane's husband, Arthur Blennerhassett of Bath, now became heir to the Ballyseedy estate.[106]

The Great Colonel John's successor in politics was a son-in-law, Arthur Blennerhassett of Arabela, the house in Ballymacelligott named for his wife, Colonel John's daughter and his own first cousin.[107] Arthur of Arabela and Rowland Bateman of Oak Park, both Shelburnite, and ambivalent on the subject of the Catholics, won election as MPs for Kerry in 1776. Their posters carried American-style slogans about democratic accountability. With Britain at war and its regular army deployed against the colonists, the two new MPs headed Volunteer companies. Colonel Arthur Blennerhassett MP headed the Ballymacelligott Corps, which included many of the Palatine community; Rowland Bateman MP commanded the Kerry Legion, "composed of shopkeepers, dealers, tradesmen", all residents of the Rock which was part of the Bateman estate.[108]

All communities suffered the effects of an embargo on trade with the colonists, and the traffic on the Butter Road to Cork ceased. France's entry into the war on the side of the colonists in 1778 reintroduced the danger of invasion, and with it a Catholic insurrection. After the visit of privateer Paul Jones to the Kerry coast, having been fitted out by the French, the *Hibernian Chronicle* reported a "Meeting of the Protestant Gentlemen, Freeholders and Inhabitants of the Town of Dingle and Neighbourhood, on the 19th of August, 1779".[109] In attendance were "several respectable Roman Catholic gentlemen" bearing a paper in which they "do hereby pledge ourselves to each other, to our Protestant fellow subjects, to our King, and to our country, that we will, to the utmost of our power, assist in repelling any hostile invasion of this kingdom by our foreign enemies". In Tralee, a Catholic chapel was constructed, the forerunner of the present St John's, when the Bishop was Francis Moylan; its construction coincided with the relief legislation of 1778 which permitted Catholics to take leases of land for 999 years. A committee of the House of Lords would later hear how the new chapel of Tralee was built "to a considerable extent with the money of the Protestants", that a monument to a popular parish priest was made possible by a large Protestant subscription, and that "the monument remains in a very conspicuous part of the Catholic chapel of Tralee."[110]

Francis Wheatley, The Volunteers on College Green 4th November 1779
(courtesy of The National Gallery of Ireland)

In the course of the war, and learning from the Americans, the Volunteers had supported the parliamentary campaign of Henry Grattan and others to win a list of concessions from Britain, including the right to trade with the West Indies. There was a Buy Irish campaign; the participants in a Fancy Ball in Tralee in February 1780 in aid of the County Infirmary wore "patriotic devices".[111] Pressure to achieve legislative independence (a modification of Poynings' Law which had restricted the right to legislate) increased from the Dungannon Convention of February 1782, and in that year Britain capitulated and granted the demand. The constitutional campaign was accompanied by the great excitement of the Volunteer reviews: Sir Barry Denny,

Colonel of the Royal Tralee Volunteers, was the County Reviewing General, and he took the salute before the assembled Corps at Clonmore in the autumn of 1782. Parliament and the Volunteers pressed the case for Catholic relief, and there is reason to believe that a former classmate of Grattan at the Middle Temple, Tralee man Robert Day, a nephew of former Dingle MP Robert FitzGerald, influenced Grattan's thinking on the Catholic question. By the Catholic Relief Act of 1782 Catholics were permitted to own land outright.

When Britain and America made peace in 1783, many Volunteers wished to continue in arms. In the 1783 elections for the County, Arthur Blennerhassett and Rowland Bateman lost their seats; many attributed their defeat to the part they played in undermining the Volunteers by becoming officers in the Fencibles. The government set up this force in the hope that it would draw support away from the Volunteers, thereby disrupting the recent consensus that had united the elite with the subjugated majority; and Arthur Blennerhassett had accepted the colonelcy of a Fencible regiment. One of his vanquishers in the general election was strongly associated with the Catholic or convert constituency: Richard Townshend Herbert of Cahernane. Yet, the public mood was turning against reform. Sir Boyle Roche MP told Parliament that his cousin Lord Kenmare had told him that the Catholics did not wish to press for further Catholic relief; but he had to retract before the resulting outcry from the Catholics could subside. It was a typical gaffe from Roche who was known for his malapropisms, or Irish bulls.

3. Tithe War and Jail Insurrection: Baptism of Fire for the Convert Party

Sir Barry Denny's Volunteer credentials helped him win a seat in Parliament for the County in 1783.[112] The convert, or Geraldine, party came to the fore in the 1783 elections and led Kerry in the coming era of revolution. Its standard bearer was John Crosbie, 2nd Earl of Glandore of Ardfert Abbey, who became County Governor in 1785. However, an equally important power behind the scenes was the Viscount Kenmare, owner of a huge estate centred on Killarney, who, because he was Catholic, could not sit in Parliament. One of the Crosbies had married a Knight of Kerry (FitzGerald) in 1703, and when the Knights were supplanted in the control of Dingle in the 1770s by the Townshends of Castletownshend, their extended family regrouped in time for the 1783 elections. Tracing their descent from the Rebel Earl of Desmond, they included the likes of MacGillicuddy (and their cousins, the Chutes of Chutehall), the powerful Hickson clan of Fermoyle (Brandon Bay), and the marriage connections of the Knight's sisters: Collis (Barrow), Hewson (Ennismore), Meredith (Dicksgrove), Marshall (Ballymacadam),

Sandes (Sallow Glen), Herbert (Cahernane) and Day (Lohercannon). Denny himself was descended from the native O'Connor clan. The coordinator of this Geraldine, or convert, interest was Glandore's legal estate agent, Tralee man Robert Day, a Dublin based barrister whose family were lease holders of the Dennys. He entered Parliament for Tuam in 1783.

Robert Conway Hickson, High Sheriff of Kerry in 1855, & his wife Jane O'Hara.
He was a cousin of the historian Mary Agnes Hickson. The Hicksons were key members of the powerful convert, or Geraldine, connection in Kerry.

Yet, the convert party shared the growing resistance to calls for reform, particularly reform of the County franchise and the opening of pocket boroughs like Tralee, Ardfert and Dingle where the party was very firmly based. Instead, it was hoped that revisiting the tithe system could do something for the poor, especially in Munster where the burden of tithe weighed most heavily. But even this was resisted in Parliament and in the Established Church, especially after the start of a new rural campaign against the tithe farmer and his hated representative in the day-to-day collection: the tithe proctor. Tralee and surrounding villages felt the full brunt of the Rightboy campaign. From 1784 we read of houses attacked for arms, breakouts from the old County Jail, chapel congregations forced to hear threats from the leaders of the insurgents, and gibbets erected by night in villages like Causeway. A poor man who defied the campaign could face *carding*, his body lacerated by the instrument used to straighten the knots in wool in preparation for spinning.

Tralee and vicinity hit the front pages of the *Dublin Evening Post* many times in the summer of 1786, most notably after of the breakout at the County Jail in August when the jailer, Patrick Hands, was murdered and his body mutilated in a manner too terrible to report. The jailer's money and his silver shoe buckles, value ten shillings, were taken; then his tormentors – the most notorious a female named Ann (Nance) Cody – crawled to freedom over the Old Jail Bridge. The government offered a reward of twenty pounds sterling each for their capture, and they were apprehended and executed over the course of the following weeks. Ann Cody feigned pregnancy to avoid the rope, but she was examined by what was described as "a jury of matrons", who found that she was not "quick with child", and so she went to her death. Her place of execution was given as the Gallows Green, but somebody later remembered it to have taken place in front of the old Jail itself.[113]

Judge Day (1746-1841), MP Ardfert 1790,
principal trustee of the Denny estate from 1795, Provost of Tralee 1797 and 1798. Despite his convert background, Day favoured progressive concessions to the Catholics (he disliked the term Emancipation), which were always to be granted in a quid pro quo for peace and good order.

The closure of America from 1783 as a destination for transported convicts, coinciding with the Rightboy campaign, may have been the torch that ignited the turmoil in the Jail. Jails received very little investment as authorities could resort to mutilations, branding, and whippings through the villages and towns where offences had occurred. Plans were afoot to substitute Australia for America, but a few more years would pass before Botany Bay would receive its first transportees. However, Tralee responded to the events of 1786 with plans to replace its old County Jail. The new structure would stand at Big River (the present Ashe Street) on the site of the present Court House. Did it commence construction too quickly after the events of that day when Cody and the others murdered Patrick Hands? Rev. Daniel Beaufort witnessed its progress during his tour of Kerry in 1788: "A new Jail now building here seems very ill contrived – the stair-cases of timber – the lower rooms dungeons with little light or air, too large for one, too small for many. No communication between the jailer's house and the Jail. The window of the cells open to the street." A second new Jail would follow within twenty years, the one whose façade can still be seen at Ballymullen.

Early in 1787 Parliament heard "A petition of the High Sheriff and Freeholders of the County of Kerry (who are) deeply affected by the general discontent and fatal riots which have … lately made their appearance in this county (and) the mode in which the revenues of the clergy are levied and collected is the ostensible reason offered as excuse of such alarming proceedings". The government response was the Riot bill of that year. An early draft contained a clause authorising the levelling of Catholic chapels where meetings had taken place, but this was deleted from the Act, which authorised whippings and fines for placing notices to advertise meetings, and for seizing arms; and the death penalty for erecting gibbets.[114] The second piece of legislation was the Magistracy Act, which introduced a new constabulary in the baronies: the Barneys.

Reformers like Henry Grattan and Tralee's Robert Day introduced measures to deal with tithe assessment and collection, including a bill that would relieve barren lands from tithe entirely, which failed to be enacted. They were aided and abetted by pamphleteers like Rev. Luke Godfrey, Rector of Kenmare. But the Established Church found many defenders who sensed that any tinkering with the system would jeopardise the Church position and the work of evangelisation that lay ahead.

4. DECADE OF THE FRENCH REVOLUTION: BARRY DENNY SHOT DEAD IN A DUEL AT OAK PARK

The outbreak of the French Revolution in 1789 brought the very limited and self-serving agenda of the Irish parliamentary opposition finally to a halt. Some months before the outbreak, King George's mental illness had returned, causing the Regency Crisis of the winter and spring of 1788/9. When the Irish opposition exploited the King's illness to raise constitutional issues about the powers of the intended regent, its leaders (Lord Shannon and others) were removed from government office. This led to the foundation of the Whig Club. However, the absentee Arthur Blennerhassett of England, son of the Great Colonel John, prepared to postpone opposition politics for now. Described as "a great Portlander", a reference to the leader of the anti-government party in England, he urged the new County MP, John Blennerhassett of Elmgrove, to support the Dublin administration.[115]

The new Catholic leadership took a more radical course. It linked its cause with that of the revolutionary United Irishmen by appointing Theobald Wolfe Tone as secretary of the Catholic Committee, and under Tone's influence the demand for new relief legislation was reactivated, with the result that in 1791 Lord Kenmare and the aristocratic old guard seceded from the Committee. Kerry rallied to the support of Kenmare, but Tone's influence as a barrister was bound to have an effect, and barristers and attorneys were perhaps the principal conduit of revolutionary separatist ideas to Tralee.

There had been hopes that the overthrow of the *ancien régime* would be bloodless and that its replacement would be a constitutional monarchy with the Bourbon dynasty still in place, but then the Revolution sent its armies into the Netherlands in 1792, and at the same time perpetrated the September Massacres against its own citizens in Paris. In the winter of 1792 a Catholic Convention was held in Dublin. Kerry sent Thomas Hussey and Matthew Moriarty as delegates; both were from Dingle. The Convention took a decision to appeal directly to George III, so a deputation crossed the Irish Sea and presented a petition to him.

In January of 1793 King Louis was executed. Count James Louis Rice of Dingle plotted to rescue his Queen, Marie Antoinette, and convey her to the Rice house in Dingle. James Louis's father, Tom, a wealthy Dingle merchant, had trade links with France and Flanders: "But Maria Antoinette pushed the idea from her. Her resolution was stronger than her misery and she said 'No, I will never abandon the King'."[116] She was executed by guillotine in the same year as her husband. The Reign of Terror followed over the next two years. The third Earl of Kerry (Francis Thomas FitzMaurice), who had been living in Paris, fled for his life to England, leaving behind his art collection which was impounded by the revolutionaries. The poor peasantry of the Atlantic Vendée suffered genocide for defending their shrines and their priests. Daniel O'Connell fled the college of the English Jesuits at Douai, where he and his brother were students, and crossed to Calais. He would become one of the first generation of Catholic barristers after the admission of Catholics to the Bar in 1792. O'Connell would later recall for a parliamentary commission how the United Irishmen in Kerry were all from the governing élite.[117] William Rowan, many times Provost, could easily have been a United man, given his circle of friends at Oxford and London in the 1780s, which included his distant cousin, Archibald Hamilton Rowan, the brothers Sheares, and the Emmets whose mother of the Emmet brothers was a Mason from Ballydowney. According to William Rowan's son, "The Emmets were his intimate associates – 'John Sheares' his personal friend, - 'Bagenal Harvey' his intimate at the Temple – of 'Curran's' unhappy home he knew many a painful anecdote from his intimacy in the House ..."[118]

England hastened efforts to prevent the extension of revolution to Ireland: the Catholic Relief Act of 1793 granted Catholic forty-shilling freeholders the right to vote. The qualification became a legal fiction: every potato garden seemed to qualify for the franchise, and what was worse, the vote had to be declared openly, so that for eighty years until the advent of the secret ballot, Kerry would witness the degrading spectacle of freeholders being driven to the poll to cast their ballots – in the presence of the landlord or his agent. The Earl of Glandore (Crosbie), who sat in the House of Lords, spoke in favour of the Relief Act; and his popularity and prestige contributed significantly to the pacification of Kerry, where he was the obvious choice to become Colonel of the Kerry Militia embodied in the same year as the Relief Act.

France was in the throes of the Reign of Terror when Sir Barry Denny was shot and killed by John Gustavus Crosbie of Tubrid in a duel at Oak Park on 20 October 1794, at about three o'clock in the afternoon. Death was instant, the ball entering his head over the left eye. Sir Barry had only recently succeeded his father on the latter's death in late April. There had been rumours that Barry senior was about to be raised to the peerage, and when Barry junior succeeded, the rumours followed him, one report giving him the title Baron Dunmore.[119] It had seemed the dawn of a new era when the new Baronet succeeded without election to the parliamentary seat in the County held by his father. The first link in the fatal chain of events leading to his death at Oak Park was another death, that of the other County MP, John Blennerhassett, of the Elmgrove family, who died suddenly at Mallow in early July. The Geraldine party decided to oppose Blennerhassett's anointed successor, John Gustavus Crosbie of Turbid, with a candidate of their own: Henry Arthur Herbert of Muckross. Crosbie was a grandson of the Great Colonel John Blennerhassett, whose daughter Mary was the wife of the candidate's father, Launcelot Crosbie of Tubrid. Herbert was an uninspired choice, but his nomination meant that there would have to be a poll, a prospect bound to provoke Crosbie and the Blennerhassetts. The campaign was a long one, and during it Crosbie fought the duel in which he killed Denny. Denny is said to have directed some of his own freeholders on how to vote, despite an undertaking to remain aloof. The contest resumed after the tragedy, continuing well past October. The *Hibernian Chronicle of* November 24 reported "the long contest" to have ended the previous Thursday. Crosbie's majority was three, reported the *Freeman's Journal* of the 25 November. Crosbie assumed his place in the Irish Parliament after taking the oath on January 28, and remained an MP until he was killed by a fall from his horse in or about the first day of July 1797 (*Hibernian Chronicle* 6 July 1797). The rumour has continued ever since that the Dennys killed him.[120]

The barrister Harman Blennerhassett, of the Killorglin Blennerhassetts and included in the entail to the Great Colonel's will, fled Ireland in 1796 having sold the Killorglin estate to Thomas Mullins of Burnham (Dingle). Harman was allied to the anti-Denny faction, the faction of Blennerhassett and its principal support, Thomas Mullins who was soon to be raised to the peerage as Baron Ventry. After the Catholics of the County constituency were enfranchised by the Catholic Relief Act, Mullins moved quickly to register as many of his tenants as he could. He hoped to make a mark in Kerry politics to reflect his weight in property, and nobody had made the strides in estate accumulation that Mullins had over recent years. Before the fatal duel, the Mullins/Blennerhassett faction achieved a head start over the more sluggish convert party represented by candidate Herbert of Muckross, whose backers, including Lord Glandore, were conspicuously slow to register the Catholics.

The appointment of a pro-Catholic Viceroy, Lord FitzWilliam, in January 1795 and the creation of a seminary at Maynooth for the formation of priests were initiatives designed to enlist Catholic support; but FitzWilliam was recalled after three months and repression ensued, particularly in the north and west of Ireland. Then the French fleet under Hoche appeared in Bantry Bay at Christmas of 1796. We will never know how loyal Munster might have proved had the fleet landed, but a storm blew up and the fleet had to leave its anchors behind and return to France. The former Bishop of Kerry, now Bishop of Cork, Dr Moylan, issued a pastoral in which he thanked God for the delivery and urged the people to remain loyal.

In 1798, when the French landed finally on the coast of Mayo under General Humbert, the Kerry Regiment of Militia was sent to oppose them – which they did with distinction. The historian/architect James Franklin Fuller wrote that his father was born during the campaign of the Kerry Militia in Mayo, "to oppose the French troops at Killala and Castlebar ... when they (the Kerry Regiment) made their last stand at Ballinamuck": "My grandmother, Elizabeth (Blennerhassett) followed her husband – at a safe distance – from place to place; and, thus it came to pass that my father was born in Carrick on Shannon when the regiment was quartered there."[121]

The French fleet was destroyed by Admiral Nelson at the Battle of the Nile in the month when the Kerry regiment confronted the French under Humbert in Mayo. In waging war on two fronts – Ireland and Egypt – the Directory had made a fatal decision to divide the war effort. Then Napoleon assumed sole control as First Consul and Edmund Burke's prophesy of a dictatorship came true.

The greatest single outrage in Kerry occurred in August when three yeomen were murdered in the barracks at Castleisland after their companions had gone to the races in Tralee and left them in charge of a quantity of arms and ammunition.

John Collis of Barrow was High Sheriff of Kerry in 1798. He was suspected of involvement with the United Irishmen when he bought timber from a member of the Arthur family of Limerick who was a known sympathiser. Collis was suspected of landing arms (in reality timber) near the Spa, and arrested, but later released.

5. THE ACT OF UNION: THE DENNYS BECOME ABSENTEES

The passing of the Act of Union of 1800 brought an economic downturn and an increase in landlord absenteeism, quite along the lines foreseen by many who opposed the Act. But significant dislocation had taken place before the Union, and for reasons unconnected with it; and by no means all of the neglect of estates can be attributed to absentees. Arthur Blennerhassett, son of the Great Colonel and heir to Ballyseedy, had moved to Bath perhaps thirty years before the Union. He had no sons. His eldest daughter, Jane, married an Englishman named George Winn, created Baron Headley in 1797, owner of a great, if scattered, estate in England. Their son, the second Lord Headley, transformed his Irish inheritance (comprising the part of the Blennerhassett estate around Aghadoe, Beaufort and Caragh Lake) to such an extent that he won the grudging admiration of Judge Robert Day, not usually an admirer of the Blennerhassetts:

> "(Headley) took an early opportunity of visiting his maternal property … & whilst every other Peer of Kerry was draining the County of its currency & produce to waste & squander in foreign climes (Lord Lansdowne, Kenmare, Ventry, even the poor Lord Branden, as well as the rich Lord Listowel) this Englishman was employed in draining the morasses & bogs of his wild estate … (with the result that) A savage & ferocious population amongst whom the King's Writ never ran nor warrant was ever executed have been metamorphosed into an orderly, well-regulated industrious Peasantry".[122]

The Dennys may have moved to live in Worcester soon after the ill-conceived renovation of Tralee Castle in 1804. Again, events of a personal rather than a political nature played a part. A trio of trustees, chief among whom was Judge Day, assumed power from the marriage of Sir Edward Denny (third Bart.) to Judge Day's daughter, Elizabeth, in May 1795, the year after the death of the groom's brother, Sir Barry, in the duel at Oak Park. After the Act of Union, Judge Day began to put the estate on a secure financial footing, as part of which he drew up the Denny Act of Parliament of 1806 which provided for the children of the new Baronet and for the young widow of his brother.[123]

The departure of the leading grandees may have gone unnoticed in the excited atmosphere of the international war, amid reports of the Kerry Militia elsewhere in Ireland, and the parades of the Trughanacmy Yeomanry in the Mall on ceremonial occasions. An Assembly Room, which had replaced the vacated Court room in the Market House in the late 1790s, held balls and soirees, and Lady Glandore, the English Countess of the owner of Ardfert, was remembered for having presided at many of these. The Windmill at Blennerville, a symbol of the increasing emphasis on tillage, made its appearance in 1801, about the same time as Judge Day's Day Place. The Windmill was the initiative of Rowland (later Sir Rowland) Blennerhassett, who suffered the tragedy of losing his wife Millicent (née Yielding) after she was blown into the machinery of the windmill and mangled. The new mail coaches made their appearance, introducing a new and sophisticated era of human transport and postal delivery.

Sir Edward Denny, 3rd Bart. (d. 1831), painted by J. Linnell in 1821,
& his wife Elizabeth Day (d. 1828), by J. Linnell

The Union of parliaments at Westminster saw the reduction of Tralee's representation to one seat, while other boroughs, including Ardfert and Dingle, were abolished entirely. The single seat became a valuable source of income for the Denny trustees, as well as the object of growing resentment among the townspeople, because, although the Relief Act of 1793 had admitted Catholics to the franchise and to the grand juries, there were no plans to move Tralee in the direction of popular democracy. The Union had promised Emancipation, and Catholic optimism was founded on the knowledge that their former oppressors would constitute but a fraction of the total membership at Westminster. Daniel O'Connell had never believed the promises and was opposed to the Union from the start, believing that the restoration of the old Irish Parliament offered a greater prospect for his country than Westminster. But there was little he could do: England had made an impressive political response to the Rebellion, and Emancipation receded even more with the resumption of the war with France; then the rebellion of Robert Emmet in the summer of 1803, coming just after the war resumed, followed by Emmet's execution in Thomas Street, Dublin, sealed the fate of the Catholic cause.[124]

Blennerville Bridge, Tralee;
postmarked 28 Jun 1913, from the W R & S Reliable Series, no. 902/4

Napoleon, who had overthrown the French Revolution, was viewed as an upstart, but he had his admirers among the poor of Tralee, and there were those among the privileged who hoped that he might bring the bloodletting in France and Europe to an end. He negotiated a Concordat with the Holy See in 1802, and he unveiled the Napoleonic Code in 1804 at a time when legal reform in England was placed firmly on the back burner. But admiration was short lived. He crowned himself Emperor and notched up an impressive series of military victories, later invading Spain. Nelson Street (today's Ashe Street) was named for the victor of Trafalgar, after which the danger of invasion receded and Wellington opened a front against Napoleon's armies in Portugal and Spain. On the high seas, relations between Britain and America continued tense as the English navy boarded American ships during the continental blockade, and then impressed American sailors for service under the flag of King George.

The public mood which so recently favoured the Volunteers now became Unionist, the convert party finding common cause with their Blennerhassett/Ventry rivals in the defence of the country and its Established Church. Gone was the old prejudice against a standing army, as Tralee became militarised beyond anything seen in the era of local and volunteer militias, and recruitment soared for the campaigns in Europe and India. Catholics had enlisted when they heard the sickening reports from their continental colleges about the genocide in the Vendée, which, added to the Revolution's treatment of the Catholic church and the aristocracy, caused the old Irish Brigade to transfer from the service of France to that of Britain. Recruitment would climb steadily to the middle of the nineteenth century, after which the rise of Irish nationalism would eclipse everything associated with Britain's Empire.

The abandonment of the country by the landed classes accentuated the difficulties in the rural areas, causing insurrection to simmer in North Kerry from about 1805. As prices rose during the wartime boom, old occupiers were cleared from the farms to facilitate rent increases; the displaced took to the road, the men becoming migrant potato diggers (*spailpíns*) in West Limerick and further afield, some settling as far away as Tipperary and Kilkenny. The iconic figure of the insurrection is James Nowlan, the *Gabha Beag* (little Blacksmith). He was sentenced to death for attempted murder but broke out of the County Jail where he was being held for execution. Recaptured, he was sent to Gunsborough for execution. There he tried to cheat death by means of a steel collar which had been smuggled into the Jail and intended to be worn at his hanging. It would have served him well, but word of the collar and its likely use were sent from the Jail to Gunsborough; his plan was foiled, and when they hanged him he died. It was April 1808. The insurrection peaked that year, and a commission in Tralee in January 1809 handed down half a dozen capital convictions; the executions took place at Gallows Green (which occupied part of the present St Brendan's Park estate) – hangings by means of a hoist.

Charles Lennox, 4th Duke of Richmond (courtesy of Goodwood Estate)

The construction of the new Barracks at Ballymullen at this time seems part of a country-wide scheme rather than an isolated response to the rural insurrection. The Viceroy, the Duke of Richmond, visited Tralee in September 1809 and announced the plans. In his speech at the Castle he promised that the Barracks would end the system of quartering the soldiers on the families of the townspeople; and he made reference to the successes of Wellesley's army in the Peninsula. Judge Day hosted Richmond's visit, and Day (the disturbances in North Kerry very much in his mind) embellished Richmond remarks with a vision of the projected barracks, "from whence a force might suddenly be brought at any time to bear upon any given point of the county".[125] In more modern times the Barracks would become the depot headquarters of the Royal Munster Fusiliers. The second *new* County Jail was constructed at Ballymullen from 1812, and it was later visited by Samuel Lewis for his *Topographical Dictionary of Ireland* (1837):

> "The County Gaol, situated near the barracks, is a large and substantial building on the radiating principle, consisting of an octangular centre containing the governor's apartments, from which project two lateral wings and one rearward containing wards for the male prisoners; in the front are two detached buildings for female prisoners and debtors, and in the rear another of semicircular form for a chapel. It affords accommodations, with separate beds, for 209 prisoners, and has a treadmill."

George Canning was returned to Westminster for Tralee for 1802-1806. The background to his nomination was as follows. He and Prime Minister William Pitt had supported Catholic Emancipation as part of the understanding with the Irish Catholics to gain Catholic support for the Union. When King George went back on his word, they resigned. Later, Pitt gave support to the anti-war and anti-Emancipation Prime Minister Addington, causing Canning to distance himself from Pitt and send himself into a long exile from the centre of politics. So Canning purchased Tralee in order to remain independent. In anticipation of finalising the purchase with Judge Day, Canning wrote: "I am determined to come into the next Parliament perfectly free and unfettered – that is by full purchase - and I am in treaty for a seat which will cost me (I am sorry to say) 4,000 gs. But it will leave me at liberty to take exactly what part I please ... In the new Parliament I have no intention ... of taking any part at all."[126] Canning sat for Tralee until 1806; he remained out of government for many years to come, fighting his famous duel with Castlereagh in 1809, and only ending his spell in the political wilderness when he joined the cabinet in 1822 on Castlereagh's death by suicide.

Sir Arthur Wellesley, the future Duke of Wellington, was returned to Westminster for Tralee in 1807. He had come to Ireland as Chief Secretary to the Viceroy, Richmond, and he was seeking at the same time a seat in Parliament. William Rowan, Provost on no less than eight occasions (1803, 1804, 1805, 1807 to 1811), had the distinction of ratifying Wellesley as MP. Rowan's son (Archdeacon Rowan) retained his father's "grey goose quill" (an eagle's quill) which he believed the Duke to have used to sign his name on the occasion.[127] In the end Wellesley declined Tralee, choosing instead Newport in the Isle of Wight. But he had reason to know Kerry well from his correspondence as Chief Secretary at Dublin Castle: it would scarcely be an exaggeration to say that while he served in that capacity the insurrection in North Kerry was his heaviest work load. Then he left one day to lead the struggle against Napoleon's armies in the Peninsula.

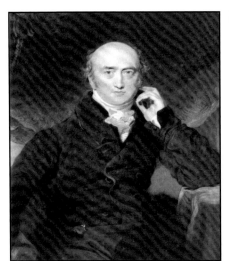 

George Canning (left) & James Stephen, MPs Tralee.

It is difficult to know what to make of James Stephen's purchase of Tralee. Stephen, the renowned anti-slavery activist, was the Tralee MP at Westminster from 1808 to 1812. He had the ear of Prime Minister Spenser Perceval, the "evangelical" Prime Minister, and the evangelical revival was the driving force behind the Protestant schools founded in Tralee in Napoleonic times. Wilberforce himself, the leading abolitionist, was Stephen's brother-in-law. Stephen exposed the breaking of the slave embargo after the abolition of the trade in slaves by the Act of 1807, and he was credited with helping Perceval to push through the Orders in Council (restricting neutral vessels in the war) to counter Napoleon's blockade at sea.[128] The agenda to defeat Napoleon supervened over all others, including Catholic Emancipation which had begun to be agitated again from 1805 when the Catholic Committee was reformed. The

Catholics were insisting on their full admission to the constitution to strengthen loyalty during wartime; however, the Tories justified the withholding of Emancipation as long as the war lasted and despite, or perhaps because of, the Catholic agitation of the question. Stephen's background as an evangelical was well known, and the evangelical movement did not look favourably on a Catholic revival, which is why his choice appears to some extent to affirm the work of the Bible societies.

A quiet revolution began in Catholic education. The Presentation sisters (in Killarney from 1793) arrived in Tralee in 1809. Mother Joseph Curtayne and Sister Mary John Sheehy were the first, and they occupied "a little rundown house in Blackpool". Cornelius Egan, Bishop of Kerry, would boast of having promoted education in Tralee "long before any free schools were established in Kerry by either the Kildare Street or Hibernian Societies, (when) I had five in Tralee, one establishment in 1809 … giving education to 500 poor children".[129] It would be another generation before the Christian Brothers established a school for boys in the town. The various Bible societies in and around Tralee received government funds through the Kildare Place Society on condition that they left aside efforts to convert the children of Catholics to the Established church. Students would sit together for most subjects and religious instruction would be given separately, with both versions of the Scriptures. The press reported a visit of educationist Joseph Lancaster to found a school in Kerry, similar to the one he had founded in Limerick.[130]

O'Connell seems to have been too preoccupied elsewhere in Ireland to interfere with the Tralee Tories. It would be said against him that he manipulated Irish insurrection throughout his rise to supreme power among Ireland's Catholics. His preferred forum was the Dublin courtroom, where the leaders of the Dublin Catholics were put on trial by the government. Between 1811 and 1813 he made his reputation in these trials, which were covered extensively in the press. One of the judges was his fellow county man Judge Day, member of the King's Bench since 1798, who frequently accused the Catholic Committee of involvement with the insurrection in the Irish regions. O'Connell countered with accusations of jury packing by the Crown. In the end it was a great division among the Catholics themselves, known as the Veto controversy, that defeated Emancipation as much as anything else: the government offered Emancipation alright, but at the price of conceding to the government a say in the appointment of bishops. One group among the Catholics was favourable to this Veto, the other opposed. A series of Tralee meetings between 1811 and 1815 opposed the Veto, probably under the influence of O'Connell.

Napoleon's retreat from Moscow in the snows of 1812 and his subsequent defeat at Leipzig led to his surrender and exile on the island of Elba. England enacted the Corn Laws to protect the farmers of England. There were protests everywhere until the news of Napoleon's escape and his reappearance on French soil. The French people flocked to him, and the Irish farmers ceased to grumble because the resumption of war raised agricultural prices; the poor of Kerry, according to Sam Hussey, cheered "Hurray for Boney who rose the (price of the) pigs".

Napoleon after the battle of Marengo, 1800, still First Consul.

International excitement coincided with excitement at home. Protest meetings in Tralee mirrored the drama in the Dublin courts in the trials of the Catholic leaders; and the Prince Regent rejected Emancipation when he appointed Lord Liverpool to govern after the assassination of Prime Minister Perceval in 1812. For now Tralee was calm. The *Cork Mercantile Chronicle* of 31 January 1812, reporting a Meeting of Roman Catholics and Friends of Religious Freedom in Tralee, has O'Connell celebrating the attendance of representatives from all the leading Protestant families. However, the reactionaries were in the ascendant in England and in Europe, and a series of Continental Congresses ensured that the political status quo would remain unchanged. Reaction began to crumble in the 1820s, then Emancipation was finally passed by a government led by the reluctant but pragmatic Wellington, by then Prime Minister.

6. THE DUEL AT BALLYSEEDY
AND THE 1818 GENERAL ELECTION

Seven weeks after Waterloo, on Monday 7 August, at Ballyseedy, a teenager by the name of Henry Arthur O'Connor was shot and injured in a duel by Rowan Cashel, an older man and a seasoned duellist. The youth lingered until Wednesday, when he died at seven in the morning. It had begun as a small argument in the town's Billiard room, and it escalated after the teenager "posted" Cashel as a coward on the gates of the Castle, Cashel having refused to *meet* the youth, instead striking him a blow. Judge Day arrived at Tralee Castle on Tuesday, the day after the shooting, accompanied by his grandson Edward Denny who was to be a candidate for the town in the next general election. It was explained to them that the shooting was the reason for the cancellation of the intended illumination prepared for the Denny heir. Next day O'Connor died, and Judge Day ordered the arrest of Cashel. The Judge's zeal to canvass for his grandson was used later by the family of O'Connor when they brought an appeal to Westminster against Day for his performance at the trial of Rowan Cashel at the Spring Assizes in Tralee in 1816. Day was extremely unwise to preside at the trial of Cashel. In court in those days, people often gave boisterous expression to their feelings: the O'Connors interrupted the summing up, and they later claimed that Day had dismissed the case because of an arrangement he had with Lord Ventry (a relative or political associate of Rowan Cashel) to receive Ventry freemen in big numbers for young Denny's election. But the Judge argued that Cashel had been provoked, and in Parliament Sir Robert Peel and Lord Castlereagh (both of whom knew Day personally) helped exonerate him against the O'Connor petition.[131] Edward Denny was indeed returned for Tralee in the general election in 1818, but the Judge resigned from the King's Bench early in 1819.

The young candidate's parents, Sir Edward and Elizabeth Denny, seem to have remained permanent absentees, but some of their sons became prominent figures in the town. These did not include the young candidate, Edward junior, who served only a year as MP and became better known as "the hymn maker". Three of his brothers kept the Denny name in Tralee: Rev. Anthony Denny, Rector of the town, Rev. Henry Denny, Rector of Churchill for 47 years, and William Denny, the youngest, who was active in the elections. The appointment of Thomas France, Solicitor, as the agent for the Denny estate, was announced in the *Kerry Evening Post* of 17 Dec. 1828. His address was given as 16 Foregate St, Worcester.

[96] *Blennerhassett Pedigree*. A deed of 1757 gave the management of the affairs of the Great Colonel to his son Arthur, pp. 67, 90; Colonel John's heir, John, predeceased him in 1763.

[97] "The post boy came but once a week, and you paid a shilling for a Dublin letter which was three or more days on the road ...". Annie Rowan in *Kerry Evening Post*, 30 Nov. 1895.

[98] Busteed brought the first printing presses to Tralee in 1774 to found the *Kerry Evening Post*. He was aided by a man called George Trinder who had Limerick connections. Busteed was the printer for Cork Corporation, a job he lost in the early 1770s, which may have precipitated his move to Tralee; see Robert Munter, *A Dictionary of the Print Trade in Ireland 1550 -1775*, New York 1988, p.43.

[99] 5 Geo 3, c. 20, An Act for erecting and establishing public infirmaries (Kerry mentioned); 7 Geo 3, c. 8 contains surgeon Murphy.

[100] *H.C. Jn. (Ir.)*, vol. 12 (1788): "Report on the state of Hospitals, Infirmaries and Public Dispensaries"; John Howard, *An Account of the Principal Lazarottos in Europe ...* (Warrington 1789), p. 91.

[101] The most celebrated of Voltaire's campaigns was his posthumous exoneration and rehabilitation of Jean Calas after Calas's execution by the *Parlement* of Toulouse on a charge of having murdered his son for turning Catholic.

[102] *H.C.*, 8 August 1774.

[103] *F. J.*, 28-31 October 1775: Parliamentary Diary, Oct.28, Major Boyle Roche.

[104] *F. J.*, 30 May-1 June 1775.

[105] Jane Blennerhassett, Bath, to her brother, Mr Ducarel, from Oak Park, near Tralee, 3 July 1774, published in *The Gentleman's Magazine*, July to December 1816. I owe this reference to the Knight of Glin.

[106] There was also an entail, in which the beneficiaries were almost exclusively those of the Blennerhassett name, including a strong cohort of the Killorglin family, notably Rev. John Blennerhassett, Rector of Tralee in the last quarter of the eighteenth century.

[107] The brothers-in-law Arthur Blennerhassett are mistakenly indentified as one and the same in Edith Johnston-Liik, *History of the Irish Parliament 1692-1800*, 2002.

[108] Archdeacon Rowan, "Tralee Seventy Years Ago", *The Kerry Magazine*, 1 January 1856.

[109] *H.C.*, 6-9 September 1779.

[110] *Report of the Select Committee of the House of Lords* 1825, Daniel O'Connell, 9 March, pp. 123-171, p.142; Bishop Moylan's predecessor, Bishop Madgett, had his residence in a little house in Strand Street, in which there was a small chapel.

[111] *H.C.*, 14 February 1780.

[112] The *Dublin Evening Post* 1 December 1789 notes that in the '83 election R.T. Herbert paid £1000 to Denny to give a Tralee seat to Godfrey "to resign his interest in the county in their (Herbert's and Denny's) favour, by that means to secure their success". Godfrey's wife was a daughter of William Blennerhassett of Elmgrove, brother of the Great Colonel John.

[113] *Kerry Evening Post*, 8 April 1868.

[114] *H.C. Jn. (Ir.)*, vol. 12 1786-88. Wednesday, 14 February, 1787; 27 Geo 3 c. 15 (The Riot Act).

[115] N.L.I., Talbot-Crosbie Ms. 2054, Robert Day to Lord Glandore, Ardfert, 6 July 1790: Blennerhassett was apparently instructed by his cousin Arthur to vote for the Government's nominee for Speaker, John Foster. The writer, Day, was returned to Parliament for Ardfert in 1790, and he is listed as Provost of Tralee in 1797 and 1798.

[116] Thomas F. O'Sullivan, *Romantic Hidden Kerry*, Tralee 1931, pp. 223-225; p. 224; the author quotes *Frazer's Magazine* of May 1865, and "Foreign Reminiscences, Lord Howard" *Edinburgh Review*, 1847.

[117] Report of the Select Committee of the House of Lords 1825; Daniel O'Connell pp.123-171, p.142.

[118] Archdeacon Arthur Blennerhassett Rowan, *Tralee and its Provost Sixty Years On, with introduction by The Last of its Provosts* (only 24 copies printed), 1860, Introduction, p.ii.

[119] Edward Flin's *Limerick Journal*, 7 April 1791; *Hib. Chron.*, 28 April 1794; *K.E.P.* 24 March 1909.

[120] *H.C.*, 6 July 1797. An earlier fatal consequence of the duel was the suicide of the father of the young widow of Sir Barry. This individual, Crosbie Morgell, a West Limerick lawyer, had helped himself to one of the Tralee seats in the Irish Parliament, but his financial prospects were dashed when his son-in-law Denny was shot dead. Morgel drowned after walking into the sea at Ringsend, Dublin.

[121] Fuller, *Omniana*, p. 21.

[122] Diary of Judge Robert Day, September 1829; Rev. William Crosbie is the fourth and last Baron Branden; Lord Listowel is Hare, of Convamore, Co. Cork.

[123] 46 George 3, cap. 142. There were no children to the marriage of Anne Morgell and Barry Denny, 2nd Bart.

[124] St John Mason, Emmet's first cousin suffered as a consequence of Emmet's rebellion: he escaped from Dublin but was later arrested, and spent his time in prison in Dublin writing letters to Lord Lansdowne, Judge Day and others, who helped alleviate his situation.

[125] What appears a verbatim report of both speeches appears in the *Freeman's Journal*, 3 October 1809.

[126] Canning papers, West Yorkshire Archives, Canning to J.H. Frere, 14 Dec. 1801.

[127] Rowan, *Tralee and its Provost*.

[128] Stephen's family owned an estate on St Christopher's. He and Zachary Macaulay were among the most able pamphleteers for abolition in their day.

[129] T.J. Walsh, *Nano Nagle and the Presentation Sisters* (Dublin 1959), p. 198; N.L.I., FitzGerald papers, Dr Cornelius Egan, Killarney, to the Knight of Kerry, March 6 1825. A plaque in Church St, Tralee commemorates the arrival in 1809 of Sr Joseph Curtayne and the other sisters.

[130] A Lancaster school existed in Dingle (Thomas F. O'Sullivan, *Romantic Hidden Kerry*, Tralee 1931, p.170); schools of the Cromwellian-era philanthropist Erasmus Smith were built on Valentia Island and in Blennerville.

[131] James F. Fuller (ed.), "Trial of Rowan Cashel, Attorney, for Murder of Henry Arthur O'Connor, Tralee, 1816", in *J.C.H.A.S.*, vols. 7 and 10 (1901 and 1904).

SIX

REVOLUTION

1. THE 1820s: GRAIN STORES APPEAR
AND TRALEE CASTLE IS DISMANTLED

Recession followed the ending of the Napoleonic War in 1815, and then, from 1816 to 1819, the country was hit by a fever epidemic. In February 1817 a mob from Tralee boarded two hookers at Blennerville and caused cargoes of corn bound for Limerick to be re-landed.[132] The Summer Assizes were postponed to the end of August to spare Tralee the arrival of crowds and the inevitable spread of infection. When the Assizes opened, the judge reviewed the "pestilential fever raging here" and how it had infected prisoners in the new and old County Jails, which were in concurrent use: "no less than twenty-six miserable bad cases in the new and old gaol".[133] Five years later, in early summer 1822, distress had made its return when the press reported: "our streets are thronged with miserable starving clamorous beggars, and swarms of naked, half-starved children ... sickness and epidemic diseases follow close on the heels of famine." By August the people of England were sending food and supplies. Francis Chute, High Sheriff, and the Grand Jury "have returned most sincere and unfeigned thanks to their fellow subjects of Great Britain and various associations formed for the relief of the suffering population of Ireland". The following day the Limerick press reported the "arrival of ships at Tralee with cargo of oatmeal for Tralee and cargo of rice for Milltown".[134]

The first quarter of the nineteenth century witnessed a sharp increase in milling and a proliferation of new grain stores in Tralee, a phenomenon greatly assisted by new road construction presided over by the famous civil engineer Richard Griffth. This is the period when Blennerville as the port of Tralee came into its own, and Griffith was among those who urged the government to support calls for the building of a canal that would link Tralee with Blennerville.[135] The Castle was now torn down to make way for the construction of Denny Street, the work of demolition presided over by the Denny agent, Billy Jack Nelligan:

> "Two of the oldest buildings in this town are now being thrown down and removed in order to present openings for new intended streets – We allude to the Old Castle of Tralee, and the remains of the Old Abbey." [136]

Some stone fragments of the Castle and some doorways are thought to have been built into houses in Denny Street. Denny Street was completed in 1834. Years later, iron railings were put in place to restrict access to the former Bowling Green: "Its (Denny Street's) flags and the adjoining demesne or green are now the promenade of every thing exclusive, or that would be so, in Tralee", reported a Dublin newspaper in February 1834.[137] The changes were not greeted with universal approval: "What crying outrage against taste, local respectability and family pride, the instrumentality of the Neligans, ... the late booby baronet perpetrated in having blotted out the Castle of his town from the topography of Kerry ..." The new Baronet, like his father an absentee, was the "the psalm-singing tasty proprietor, Sir E. Denny".[138] Some significant features of the old town remained, including the uncovered river:

"On either side of the river were narrow streets. Thatched houses abounded, but were varied with a few more important slate roofs ... One small church and one chapel sufficed for religious instruction....[139]

Chimney piece, Tralee Castle. "In the possession of Francis McGillycuddy Denny, of 17 Denny Street, Tralee. These pieces of stone are carved with the Denny arms and motto (with the Baronet's Hand), and two with the crest, forming parts of a chimney piece once in Tralee Castle. Given him by Mr Neligan of Churchill, who found them somewhere about the Central Hotel, Denny Street." (Diary of the Rev. Sir Henry Lyttelton Lyster Denny)

The activity at Blennerville port signalled a rejuvenation of the butter trade, and from 1824 the press was reporting new market facilities in Tralee for butter and linen. Both markets were said to be crowded on Saturdays. A meeting chaired by the Provost sent a memorial to the Lord Lieutenant seeking a grant to rebuild the Quay and erect a Pier.[140] A new Weigh House was intended to exploit the possibilities of the port, reducing and eventually abolishing the old charge for transferring the butter in firkins by pony to the port of Cork. In September it was reported:

"No less than 600 firkins of butter were bought up in our market last week ... A vessel wholly laden with butter is now in our harbour on the eve of sailing, being the first instance of the kind which has yet occurred... Our Linen Market is much crowded and in full operation this day."[141]

A "Mr Cox of London" seems to have spearheaded the change, having "taken in perpetuity that ample lot and concern at Blennerville, including the very large store at the south end of Blennerville-Bridge and Wind Mill, together with the long-extended line of Quayage between the two edifices last mentioned for the purpose of erecting the necessary buildings and for carrying on the Slaughtering, Butter and Corn export provision trade, on the most extensive scale".[142]

The executions of convicted prisoners now took place from a drop in front of the new Jail. This is how Darby Buckley was executed in 1820, "hanged at the drop of the new Jail, in Tralee, for the murder of his first cousin". The same drop was pressed into service again, shortly before the elections riots of 1826 (below), for the execution of Johanna Lovett. People said it was the first execution of a female since Nance Cody, which was exactly forty years before. Johanna Lovett died "in the view of an immense multitude of spectators", having been convicted for her part in the murder of her husband.[143] Then the Jail took delivery of the treadmill seen by Lewis. Judge Jebb is reported to have called for one in 1824,[144] and its installation was reported in the *Kerry Evening Post*, 21 March, 1829: "A tread mill, on a most effectively operative plan and scale, has been received at our County Jail a few days since, and is now in progress of perfect completion." A historian of the Cork-Kerry border region has written: "The Tralee Assizes were bad news in our side of the country. They reeked of injustice, and through a backup service of spies and informers could send people to prison and death virtually at will." It was the era of the Rockites. Captain Rock was Thady Cotter who was convicted in front of Jebb and Vandeleur in 1824, and later hanged at Shinagh Cross, Rathmore.[145]

A new Court House in the classical style was completed in 1835 to the design of William Vitruvius Morrison. When the construction began by clearing away the old Jail, the workmen found the remains of the nine men executed in 1809; they had been buried in the yard of the Jail and quicklime scattered on their bodies. The Mall seems covered over by 1844, if we are to interpret William Denny's testimony before the Devon Commission that year, though John O'Donovan's Name Books of about the same time record Day Place still separated from Staughton's Row by the Big River.

The campaign for Emancipation revived suddenly to lift the spirits of the people. The Pope had issued a bull in 1820 condemning Bible societies; and among the poor the prophecies of Pastorini, forecasting the destruction of the Established Church, spread like wild fire. In 1823 O'Connell rejuvenated the movement by founding the Catholic Association (replacing the banned Committee), for which he enlisted the support of the masses by the ingenious strategy of taking a small regular subsidy from as many as could pay: the Penny Rent. A controversy with the Bible societies around schooling buried the old internal divisions between O'Connell and the likes of Richard Lalor Shiel from the days of the Veto constrovesy. The work of the Bible societies gathered pace in the 1820s in the so-called Second Reformation, with the government continuing to disburse funding through the Kildare Place Society. One of the recipients of funds was Judge Day's school on Strand Street, founded in the early 1820s and bearing the date and the name of the founder above the doorway entrance.[146] There was mounting criticism of the Society from the Catholics, headed by O'Connell, and isolated controversies involving clergymen of opposing denominations broke out in places like Killorglin and Ardfert.

Major Collis was murdered on 21 Nov. 1821 at his home, Kent Lodge, near Spa, and Baron Pennefather later sentenced two men to death and one to transportation. The circumstances of Major Collis's murder - shot a dozen times in the body, robbed of money and his wife threatened to not summon assistance - appalled the region. Over in Meanus (near Castleisland) Francis Drew built up the windows of his house to protect his family.[147]

2. THE LAST PROVOST: THE O'CONNELLS RECLAIM THE CHARTER

"This place belongs to the Denny family, and is perhaps the only one mentioned in a marriage settlement as a provision for the younger branches of the proprietor."
(*The Times* of London, 16 June 1829)

The rise of the democrats was helped by revolution in Europe and South America from 1820. Canning's return to government in 1822 was another positive indicator, foreshadowing his spell as prime minister in the year of his death, 1827. In Ireland, Catholic supporters began to occupy jobs under the state, including the judiciary. In Kerry the Tory hegemony began to crumble from the 1826 County election, which produced a near-revolution at the poll in Tralee when a banner or banners heralded "O'Connell and Independence". A reactionary cartel of Lord Ventry, Blennerhassett and the new power of Hare (purchaser of the FitzMaurice estate) attempted to thwart a "Catholic" attack on the second seat, by organising their freemen as never before and marching them to Tralee to poll for young William Hare. The first seat was retained by the Knight of Kerry, Maurice FitzGerald, who, despite a long record of support for the Catholics, was seen now as part of the anti-reform and aristocratic cartel. For the second seat, John O'Connell of Grena, brother of *the Liberator*, seconded the candidacy of Colonel Crosbie of Ballyheigue, the crowd favourite. There were "inflammatory speeches and harangues" as Major Mullins, of the Ventry family, and Blennerhassett were shouted down by a Crosbie mob. The Tory press reported an "open and avowed system of murder and bloodshed" for the violent reception afforded the visiting freemen from the Ventry and Hare estates, who were "to be deterred from the exercise of their elective franchise".[148] First, the mob advanced to Blennerville to confront the freemen, then serious violence ensued on the streets of Tralee, and in Nelson (Ashe) St five people were shot. Hare defeated Crosbie. For now the Tories had won a lease of life.

James Cuff Esq., son of Lord Tyrawley, of Co. Mayo, was the Tralee representative at

Westminster since 1819. When he died near the end of July 1828, the news and the prospect of an O'Connell candidacy spread mild panic through the town oligarchy. "Dan the Liberator, the Agitator General, threatens to enact the farce of Clare at Tralee", wrote Judge Day in his diary, a reference to O'Connell's simultaneous campaign to win election for Co. Clare.[149] As Cuff lay dying, O'Connell seems to have bid £3000 to purchase the Tralee seat, but the offer was rejected and O'Connell went on to take the seat in Clare as the choice of the Clare electorate. A candidate was ready to fill the shoes of Cuff in Tralee: the absentee patron himself, Sir Edward Denny. Through August the town oligarchy prepared to ratify Denny, which it duly did on 12 September, though not without the very "farce of Clare" which the oligarchy had feared. The Court House was the venue for the election, the Provost, Captain Caleb Chute, presiding. Denny had not travelled from his home near Worcester to be present, and nobody seems to have expected that he would. The O'Connell-ites put up a candidate in the person of Nicholas Philpot Leader, Esq. "of the County of Cork", who, if he was present, does not appear in the press reports. But Provost Chute refused to entertain either Leader's proposer or seconder, both of whom were residents of the town, and declared Sir Edward elected. John O'Connell, the brother of the Liberator, then "insisted upon the right of the inhabitants of Tralee to vote at the election by virtue of the Charter", and when his words had no effect he and his supporters announced their intention to send a petition to Westminster. Rev. Arthur Blennerhassett Rowan used "false" to describe John O'Connell's assertion that the burgesses had given up their rights to their absentee patron; in response to the taunt, John O'Connell "expressed his contempt for the Rev. gentleman", hinting that if the words had come from a layman, his response would have been a physical one.[150]

Emancipation was considered to have been achieved when O'Connell was permitted to take his seat at Westminster as MP Clare, yet the supremacy of the Tralee oligarchy and the Denny trustees remained unbroken in the succeeding elections. Robert Vernon Smith, of Savile Row, Middlesex, was returned for Tralee in June 1829 and again in 1830. Smith came from "the noble family of Carrington, of which there are at present, as we are informed, eight members serving in the present Parliament", according to the *KEP*, 10 June, 1829. He was a nephew of Sydney Smith, founder of the *Edinburgh Review* and author of the *Plymley Letters* which put the case for Catholic Emancipation. None of these impeccably Whig credentials impressed the democrats of Tralee however, who petitioned Parliament against Smith.[151] The petition stated that "the said usurped right" (to sell the representation) rested on "the intermarriage of the present Sir Edward Denny, Baronet, with the daughter of Robert Day, Esq." and that "Robert Day, Esq., and Stephen Edward Rice, Esq., of Mount Trenchard, in the county of Limerick … are parties to the aforesaid marriage settlement".

The Reform Parliament 1833, by George Hayter (session of 5 February 1833).
O'Connell leans forward front row right. Peel is eighth to O'Connell's right, same row; Gladstone is
in the row behind O'Connell. Courtesy of the National Portrait Gallery

In the end, the catalyst for change was the overthrow of Wellington, Peel and the Tories in 1830 by the Whigs under Earl Grey, a ministry which included the Kerry magnate Henry Petty-FitzMaurice, third Marquess of Lansdowne. Under Earl Grey the great Reform Law was passed in 1832, and for the general election at the end of 1832 Maurice O'Connell, son of the Liberator, was chosen to oppose the latest Denny, the psalm singing and apolitical Sir Edward, 4th Bart. The Liberator himself had unseated his old ally Maurice FitzGerald, the Knight of Kerry, to take the County for himself in the previous year, and this generated great bitterness. In the campaign to elect his son, charges of widespread intimidation were levelled against the O'Connell machine, which may have learned lessons from the London mob after the passage of the Reform bill during the summer, when Wellington was almost dragged from his horse as he rode out from Apsley House:

"Every country town is a hotbed of sedition capable of being permeated at any moment at the dictate of O'Connell, who now acts through a systematic organisation having its branches everywhere … the humble voter is deprived of all independence by a tyranny menacing his personal safety and compromising all the fruits of his industry… For the town of Tralee we shall endeavour to get Sir Edward Denny, a strict conservative, but we have [great] difficulties. O'Connell's son is his competitor and the lowering of the town franchise embarrasses us."[152]

In the course of the canvass Maurice O'Connell challenged one of the Denny supporters, Arthur Blennerhassett of Ballyseedy to a duel, which took place "at a spot near the turnpike on the Killarney road", but, though shots were fired, nobody was injured and the seconds intervened. The conservative press reported it all in detail, including the priestly organization that was the backbone of the O'Connell machine, what one newspaper called "a priest, armed with the powers of this world and the next". The poll took place a week or so before Christmas. Fr John McEnery was the proposer for Maurice O'Connell, who won the seat comfortably over Sir Edward.[153]

The defeated Tories of Tralee departed to Denny Street to their newly-founded County Club. Would they, or could they, regroup? The Liberator, confident of the Whigs, negotiated a pact with Earl Grey's successor, Melbourne, that lasted the rest of the decade.

This, then, was the electoral background to the visit of the parliamentary commissioners who arrived in Tralee in October 1833 to examine the workings of the Corporation for their report on the Municipal Corporations in Ireland. The inquiry was held in the town on 16 and 17 October 1833.[154] The report acknowledged that for the first time a popular candidate (Maurice O'Connell) had unseated the Corporation's candidate for Parliament, but that in municipal affairs the old restrictions continued in operation: the Corporation was a self-replacing body, its membership free of the obligation to reside, and composed exclusively of members of the Denny family and their associates.

The O'Connells continued to win the Tralee seat in the general elections. In 1837, the *Limerick Chronicle*, hardly unbiased, described the O'Connell party as "truly the mock friends of civil and religious liberty and freedom of election, who seem to think themselves entitled by patent right to use every species of scurrility and brute force to their opponents", reporting also "a cowardly and murderous attack on Mr. Bateman's Committee Rooms, of which the windows were smashed in with stones, and several gentlemen beaten, injured and abused".[155] Once again Fr John McEnery nominated Maurice O'Connell, while William Denny, who lost narrowly to O'Connell in the 1835 general election, introduced his opponent, John Bateman. Bateman defeated O'Connell (75 to 64), but on petition Bateman was unseated and O'Connell declared elected; the result was amended the following March: O'Connell 133, Bateman 111. A subscription funded the appeal, the grounds for which were stated as "the extraordinary conduct of the returning officer (in) the decision by which over 100 of the respectable and independent constituency of this borough have been disfranchised".[156] In 1841 Maurice O'Connell was returned without a contest, likewise in 1847 when he was again proposed by Fr McEnery, who had to defend his candidate against repeated accusations of non-attendance at Westminster.

William Denny as a boy, by John Linnell, 1821 at Worcester.
He was the youngest son of Sir Edward Denny. He failed to defeat Maurice O'Connell in the 1835 general election to regain the town seat for his family. He became Provost of Tralee in 1838 and died in 1871.

What of O'Connell's achievements at Westminster during the Whig hegemony of the 1830s? O'Connell's arrangement with the Whigs under Lord Melbourne, known as the Lichfield House compact, postponed calls for repeal, and provided for his cooperation with the ministry to pass a raft of reform legislation. It was undoubtedly a successful coalition but it should be remembered that his principal allies were liberal unionists from his own western region of Ireland, including Thomas Spring Rice, of Mount Trenchard, Co. Limerick, whose forebears were from Kerry and who knew Tralee well from inspection visits to the County Jail. Spring Rice played an important role in introducing the national schools, which represented the latest effort to get all denominations sharing the same educational system. Also at Westminster was the great historian Macaulay, and radical Whigs like Brougham, not to mention all of

O'Connell's old rivals from the days when he had no forum but the courts and the press, such as Wellington and Peel. In the national schools the decline of the Irish language was speeded up, and in this respect O'Connell seems to have been a true Whig. He had little interest in the Irish language, unlike his rivals and successors in Young Ireland, and the *tally stick* was worn around a pupil's neck with notches for every time the pupil used Irish, with chastisement to follow. As parish priests everywhere took over the boards, Rev. Arthur Rowan complained that the original non-denominational character of the national schools was being overthrown (with the government capitulating to the likes of the Archbishop of Tuam, John MacHale). Rowan was less inclined to blame the Whigs for the debacle, preferring to blame some of his own church's hierarchy, such as Archbishop Whately of Dublin who winked at what was happening.[157]

The controversy surrounding the payment of tithes to the Protestant minister was finally resolved by the legislation of 1838, and in the same year the complexion of local government was altered completely with the passing of the Poor Law for Ireland, under whose terms a workhouse was built in Tralee and the County divided into poor law unions. The Tralee workhouse was opened on 1 February 1844, near Rathass on the site of the later County Hospital and the present County Council offices.

The removal of the old Corporation was provided for in the Municipal Corporations Act of 1840, completing the work of the commission that had visited Tralee seven years before. The last Provost, the future Archdeacon Arthur Blennerhassett Rowan, was gracious in the act of handing over Tralee to the new Town Commission:

"In the month of October, 1841, my father, Archdeacon Blennerhassett Rowan, Archdeacon of Ardfert, and the Burgess men resigned the care of this town into the hands of the newly appointed Town Commissioners."[158]

3. ANTICIPATING THE GREAT FAMINE

Tralee was visited by some considerable health catastrophes in the decades before the Great Famine of the 1840s. The Asian Cholera epidemic of 1832 reached Kerry with terrible effect, its symptoms dramatic dehydration and rapid death; then it travelled across the Atlantic to affect our exiles in North America.

What infrastructural arrangements were in place to provide for these crises? A new infirmary was in operation since about 1793, the approximate date of William Crumpe's appointment as infirmary physician. He and his remarkable son, Francis, dominated Tralee medicine for two generations, their careers spanning an era of over seventy years from the turn of the nineteenth century through the Asian Cholera epidemic of 1832 to the Great Famine, and the succeeding twenty years. Francis succeeded William when William died in 1821, remaining at the Infirmary for fifty years, becoming also physician to the County Jail where he succeeded Rickard O'Connell in 1830 in time for the Cholera epidemic.[159] Mention might be made of Thomas Mawe M.D. who is listed in *Holden's Directory* of Tralee in 1811 and *Pigot's* of 1824. Is this the Dr Thomas Mawe whose death appears in the press during the Cholera epidemic?

"His incessant attendance at the Hospitals – from the commencement and during the period of the epidemic – together with his very successful practice on many private cases, caused a state of debility predisposing him for a death so sudden and so melancholy."[160]

District Veterinary Officer, East End

When the worst was over, one observer believed that the Cholera epidemic was the instrument of God, "with which it has pleased Him to scourge the whole World for their sins". As it ended, it was succeeded by another "much more general than the other but comparatively of a mild character", called "Influenza".[161]

Sir Robert Peel, Prime Minister from 1841 to 1846, had an old Tralee associate in Anne, Lady Denny, widow of the young man killed in the duel at Oak Park. She became Lady Denny Floyd when she married General Sir John Floyd in 1805. She and a daughter from Floyd's previous marriage appear to have met Peel at some official function in Dublin at the time when General Floyd was serving in Ireland and Peel was Chief-Secretary. Lady Denny Floyd arranged for Peel to visit the Floyd home in London, in this way providing the occasion for the renewed acquaintance of Julia Floyd and Peel and for their romance to begin in earnest. They were married in June 1820. It was Peel who introduced the Emancipation bill in 1829, then famously split the Tories by repealing the Corn Laws when he regained office as PM in 1841, in time for the Irish Famine.

Archdeacon Rowan had met Peel in London at Lady Denny Floyd's house when a young clergyman in the early 1820s. Now, as the Great Famine took its terrible toll on the countryside surrounding Tralee, Rowan had reason to survey Peel's performance in famine relief measures, as well as in measures that threatened their common Established Church. Rowan was very active in alleviating distress during the Famine, but he had suffered a blow to his reputation when the Tralee Savings Bank, founded in 1823, collapsed sensationally in 1848. Rowan was a director of the bank and many held him responsible for failing to supervise the secretary, who admitted misappropriation of its funds.[162] He had better success as chairman of the Harbour Commission when it built Tralee's ship canal. It was constructed through the 1830s and was finally opened in 1846 (Lewis, author of the *Topographical Dictionary*, noticed its construction in 1836, as "the canal which is now in progress").

In the early 1840s, O'Connell brought his campaign for repeal of the Union to a climax with a succession of *monster* meetings to pressure his old adversary, now Prime Minister. Though he had the priests as usual in support, and the support also of Fr Matthew, the temperance priest from Tipperary, Peel never forgot his old conflict with O'Connell (perhaps in particular their abortive duel in 1815). O'Connell was sentenced to a spell in prison when he defied the government over one of his *monster* meetings (none of which took place in Kerry), and when he emerged from prison he was a weakened man.

Peel attempted moderation with two initiatives in 1845. One was the setting up of the Queen's Colleges – which included the University Colleges in Cork and Galway; the other was the augmentation of the grant to Maynooth College and the removal of the need for an annual debate on the grant, with the provision to have it paid out of the consolidated fund. But O'Connell declared his hostility to what he called the "godless colleges", and the government received little credit for its initiative on Maynooth; instead, the Oxford Movement, associated with Cardinal Newman, began making steady inroads into the Established Church, a situation which provoked Rev. Arthur Blennerhassett Rowan at his home in Belmont, Ballyard, to wield his pen in pamphlets in defence of his Church, in one of them stating that Puseyism was "eating deep into the vitals of our Church", whose young men were being "perverted to Romanism".[163]

4. THE GREAT FAMINE

The Whig, Lord John Russell, was Prime Minister for most of Ireland's Great Famine, having succeeded Peel in 1846. Under Russell's Soup Kitchen Act of early 1847, food distribution committees were organised throughout Kerry. Lord Ventry and his wife kept a large boiler at their own expense constantly at work distributing free soup to the starving poor.[164] In Dingle the recently formed conference of the St Vincent de Paul organisation made an important contribution, while nearer Tralee Rev. Arthur Rowan ran a soup kitchen in the parish of Kilgobbin (Camp), to which he had recently moved on being appointed Rector and where he joined his efforts with those of the Parish Priest of Castlegregory.[165] The Poor Law Amendment Act 1847 greatly expanded the role of the Poor Law unions, placing them for the first time in charge of famine relief and permitting the distribution of relief outside, as well as inside, the workhouse. The Tralee Union covered the entire Dingle peninsula. Yet, the Union workhouse, on the site of the later County Hospital in Tralee, must have been the centre of intense activity, the place that carried the brunt of the distress. The infamous (Gregory) *Quarter Acre* Clause, included in the Amendment Act, reflected the current economic downturn in England and the Whig's debt to their working-class support in the recent election; in order to avail of relief, an applicant must surrender his holding in order to come under the threshold at which relief could be given. In April 1847 a visitor to Tralee was informed that local distress was "quite beyond their means of relief" even though the town was situated on the estate of "a rich, unencumbered landlord who draws about £12000 a year out of it but whose subscribtion for the relief of his starving tenants was paltry in the extreme".

> "While I write this note, there is a child about fire years old lying dead in the main street of Tralee opposite the windows of the principal hotel, and the remains have lain there several hours on a few stones by the side of a footway like a dead dog."[166]

Assisted emigration to the United States and Canada had begun well before the Famine as part of measures to clear landlord estates of excess population. Blennerville, and later Cork when the railway facilitated travel there, began to take huge numbers as the Famine took its toll, with money from the Board of Guardians providing the necessary assistance.

5. YOUNG IRELAND AND THE TRALEE ELECTION OF 1852: THE TRALEE TORIES STAGE A COMEBACK

Young Ireland grew out of dissatisfaction with the alliance of O'Connell with the Whigs during the 1830s and the failure of his peaceful campaign for Repeal of the Act of Union of the early 1840s. O'Connell died in 1847. Young Ireland's lasting achievement was its long-running newspaper, *The Nation*, edited by Charles Gavan Duffy. There, in poetry and prose, they recovered the glory of Ireland's past, particularly the eras of the Celts and the Christian culture that followed. William Pembroke Mulchinock found an outlet for his poetry in *The Nation*, before departing for America with his young family in the immediate aftermath of the Famine.

It is believed that his marriage failed and that he returned and found love with a poor girl, Mary O'Connor. He is the supposed writer of *The Rose of Tralee* in memory of Mary, who is said to have died young. In America he dedicated a volume of his poems to Henry Wadsworth Longfellow, and individual poems to Ralph Waldo Emerson and Henry Clay. Emerson and Washington Irving appear on his list of patrons. The poems themselves place him in the tradition of Gerald Griffin, William Allingham and others who anticipated the Irish Literary Revival of a generation later.

The less remarkable achievement of Young Ireland remains the insurrection of 1848. They were naïve revolutionaries, in the tradition of the nineteenth-century romantics, and their insurrection took place during the Irish Famine, though against the background of the Year of Revolutions in Europe; it fizzled out at the Widow MacCormack's Cabbage Garden in Tipperary. Maurice Leyne of Tralee was with the Tipperary insurgents; his grave stone in Thurles tells that he "he played his part gallantly and was at last arrested with Meagher and O'Donoghue near Holy Cross", by which is meant the place of that name in Tipperary.

O'Connell is dead by the time of the 1852 election. Dead also are his old adversaries, Peel (1850) and the Duke of Wellington (1852). Judge Day is long dead. The Judge's son-in-law, Sir Edward Denny, never made a mark; he was an absentee from perhaps 1810 and died in 1831, so his mantle fell on the shoulders of some of his sons.[167] The dominant Tory influence in Tralee for many years was Rev. Arthur Blennerhassett Rowan, but William Denny was to the fore when the oligarchy attempted to regain the Tralee seat in the general election of 1852 from the Liberal/Repeal party of O'Connell. Rev. Rowan had softened his outlook since the days when he tried to resist the O'Connell campaign to take Tralee in 1832. Back then the *Dublin Magazine* described him walking around Tralee "with all the parsonic confidence of future canonisation".[168] With the parliamentary seat lost, and the borough opened up, Rev. Rowan continued to be associated with the oligarchy as it squared up for a rematch: the *Tralee Chronicle* of June 1852 designated him "Rev. Arthur Rowan, that stage divine who pulls the wires of the Conservative puppet show".[169] The candidate chosen by the oligarchy to unseat Maurice O'Connell, son of the Liberator, was George Herbert Kinderley, described as a Lincoln's Inn attorney.

The Prime Minister was the Tory Lord Derby, formerly Stanley, the Irish Chief-Secretary of thirty years before. Derby succeeded Lord John Russell whose Ecclesiastical Titles bill was passed into law in 1851 in reaction to the Pope's decision to re-establish the Catholic hierarchy in England. "Papal aggression" was the slogan of the time. The Derby government prohibited Catholic processions after anti-Catholic riots at Stockport. During the Tralee election campaign the Liberal/Repeal party saluted Young Ireland leaders William Smith O'Brien and Charles

Gavan Duffy, and references were made to the recent Famine, "an ordeal of famine, pestilence, and bitter privations".[170] Another election audience heard Maurice O'Connell refer to the Stockport riots: "Lord Derby was called Proclamation Stanley in 1830 and 1831" (a reference to the Coercion act of that time). "Is he not Proclamation Derby in 1852?"[171] Kinderley seems to have visited the town only once, where he had this to say about the election practices: "They were employing – I believe I am right in saying – ten or twelve people to bribe, some without the slightest discretion … It is scarcely a figure of speech to say that they were bribing in the market place at noonday."[172] In the end, Maurice O'Connell retained his seat, and when he died the following year he was succeeded by his brother Daniel.

The town's appearance had changed once again. The Victorian aspect, so familiar in the twentieth century, had begun to take shape, with Castle Street and the Mall now dominated by the shop fronts, all tending to eclipse the Georgian quarter at Day Place. The river was covered over, and only a bollard remains today to remind of where small vessels used to dock at the town Quay. Archdeacon Arthur Rowan (+ 1861) listed the great changes of his twilight years: the telegraph, the railway (bringing Tralee within the range of a seven hour journey of Dublin), finally the steam packet – sailing from Tralee port direct to Liverpool and London. Tralee was no longer the "obscure village" of his youth under the shadow of the Castle. The principal new technology of the 1850s was the telegraph. It brought the news of Britain's disasters in the Crimean War. In a few years the Atlantic Telegraph Cable would send signals across the Atlantic from a station on Valentia Island. The train and the telegraph became indispensable features of electioneering from this time on.

6. BISHOP DAVID MORIARTY:
THE ECCLESIASTICAL LANDSCAPE OF TRALEE TAKES SHAPE

David Moriarty came to Tralee as coadjutor Bishop of the diocese in 1854, the same year the railway reached Killarney, the same year Britain went to war against Russia in the Crimea. By time the railway reached Tralee in 1859 Britain had suffered the India (Sepoy) Mutiny, which compelled the Crown to take over the governance of India from the East India Company. The calamities in India and the Crimea were the inspiration for the committee of the Kerry War Testimonial, which, having received a gift of two Russian Trophy Cannon, agreed finally with the townspeople a site for their erection, together with the inscribed names of Tralee men who had served in India and the Crimea. They are still to be seen on their plinths in front of the Court House.

Lord Palmerston became Prime Minister in February of the year following Moriarty's arrival in Tralee, assuming office with a powerful mandate to extricate Britain from the Crimean War, where the atrocious conditions endured by the soldiers had shocked people at home in England and Ireland. Bishop Moriarty's championship of Catholic education would draw little support from Palmerston (though the PM had a huge Irish estate around Sligo); instead, Moriarty drew inspiration from the stand taken by the current Pope, Pius IX, who condemned revolution in Italy and liberalism in France for their attacks on the educational programme of the Catholic church. Moriarty had experienced the 1848 revolutions in Europe, and he had come to Kerry from Dublin where he was president of All Hallows College and a friend of Archbishop Paul Cullen. Cullen is the name most associated with the devotional revolution in Ireland at this time; Moriarty would invite the Redemptorist Order to give their huge parish missions in Tralee, but he would not share Cullen's support for Papal infallibility, returning home early from Rome rather than vote for it. Moriarty settled first in Tralee where Fr Mawe vacated his own rooms and placed them at his disposal.

Moriarty brought exceptional experience from Dublin where he was a friend of John Henry Newman. When the future Cardinal Newman came to Dublin as head of the new Catholic University, Moriarty was his principal supporter. Now in Tralee, Moriarty made a tour to his native region just north of Tralee. He visited Ardfert classical school (where he had probably been a pupil). Then he set about his great work of introducing additional religious orders involved in education, and reintroducing the old regulars, the Dominicans and Franciscans friars so long associated with Tralee and Killarney respectively. The year he arrived in Tralee, he introduced the Mercy sisters (foundress Catherine Macauley), whose first school was a house in Day Place. In 1855 the Christian Brothers (in Dingle since 1848) came to Tralee, having been applied for by Moriarty, despite the reservations of Dean Mawe who feared the additional burden on the townspeople. John Mulchinock, a convert to Catholicism, helped both the Brothers and the Sisters, providing the Brothers with rooms in a house in Day Place and later with land for them and the Sisters at Balloonagh, which he had purchased from the Bateman estate under the Encumbered Estates Act. The commission of 1855[173] heard that the CBS in Tralee had been opened that very May.

The railway station was opened in Tralee in 1859; the Dominicans returned to the town in 1861 and the foundation stone for the new Holy Cross was laid by Bishop Moriarty in 1866. The new St John's was completed in 1870.

The Phoenix Society, which spread from West Cork in the late 1850s, was a precursor to the Fenians (Irish Republican Brotherhood). When members of the Phoenix Society were tried in Tralee in April 1859, the packing of the juries to ensure convictions drew the ire of all shades of opinion, including that of Bishop Moriarty. When Queen Victoria and her consort Prince Albert arrived at Muckross House in 1861, Britain had been chastened by her experience in the Crimea and in India. Prince Albert was enjoying some vindication for having consistently opposed as reckless the Crimean adventure when the press and the populace clamoured for it. None of this impressed the Fenians. Victoria's and Albert's visit was happening at the high watermark of Victorian imperial and commercial pride; and though Britain was seen to be enthusiastic for the liberation of subject peoples abroad in Europe, she displayed a great reluctance to grant similar liberation to Ireland.

Bishop David Moriarty (Daniel McSweeney collection)

What made the Fenian Brotherhood different from its predecessors was that many of its members had experience in the American Civil War, from which they filtered quietly back to Ireland and England when it was over – more usually to England where they could enjoy some anonymity. They would also exploit the propaganda opportunity given by high-profile funerals, and it was the issue of funerals that drew them into conflict with the Catholic Church: there was conflict over the funeral of Terence Bellew McManus in 1861, and the funerals of John O'Mahony and Charles Kickham.[174]

In 1863 the Liberator's son, Daniel junior, suddenly resigned his Tralee seat and arranged for Thomas O'Hagan, the current Attorney-General, to succeed him at Westminster. The Conservatives were wrong-footed by the suddenness of the move and they alleged that the seat had been sold in a "clandestine arrangement between Mr O'Connell and the Government". O'Hagan came to Tralee for the nomination, which took place in the Court House, and by the time of his arrival, William Denny, who had been hastily drafted to oppose him, had conceded victory. Conservative allegations against O'Hagan were economical with the truth, saying that he knew nothing of the needs of the town, such as a pier at Fenit and improvement of the harbour, and a rail link to Tralee. They ignored O'Hagan's career in the courts, where he had acted for Gavan Duffy, and he had a particular interest in the National schools, serving from 1858 on the Board of National Education. He identified with the Catholic cause throughout his rise in the legal world, and he became the first Catholic to be appointed Lord Chancellor.[175]

Thomas O'Hagan (left), 1st Baron O'Hagan, and Daniel O'Donoghue of the Glens, MPs Tralee.

In 1865 O'Hagan left Tralee to become a judge of the common pleas. In his place Tralee returned Daniel O'Donoghue, otherwise *The* O'Donoghue of the Glens, grand-nephew of O'Connell, the Liberator. He was a flamboyant figure, and politically volatile. This is not to deny his real achievements. The O'Donoghue had flirted with Fenianism just a few years earlier while MP for Tipperary when the American Irish tried to sow the seeds of Fenianism in Ireland. He was, by 1859, "the recognised leader of the independent oppositionists inside and outside Parliament", and in the following year he was part of the deputation that met Marshal MacMahon in France to present that worthy with a sword, hoping that MacMahon would agree to become Ireland's king. He had a meeting with John Mitchel at Boulogne in 1861. During his Tralee election campaign he claimed the mantle of his famous relative as the exponent of civil and religious liberty. He made a great impression when he assisted George Day Stokes to run the first race meeting at Stokes's Mount Hawk, repeating the impression in April of the following year.[176] However, his continued support for the Fenians after election earned him the suspicion of the government and the public censure of Bishop Moriarty.

Early in 1867 the Fenians destroyed the overland telegraph wires leading to Cahirciveen, and the staff was warned not to repair the breaks. As a result, the telegraph station so recently established on Valentia Island for communicating with Newfoundland, was rendered useless.

7. THE FOUNDING OF HOME RULE, AND THE FAMOUS BY-ELECTION OF 1872

Gladstone came to power in 1868 with the mission to pacify Ireland. He embarked immediately on the Disestablishment and disendowment of the Anglican Church; then, in 1870, he passed the first of the Land Acts. As far as the unionists were concerned the Prime Minister was capitulating to the Fenians. Disestablishment, which took effect from 1871, remained an open sore for years to come, and although the Dennys received considerable monetary compensation from Disestablishment, one observer opposed the use of her Church's wealth to endow Maynooth College: "the proposed application of the church surplus to the endowment of a department of the Roman Catholic Church, and the destruction of the Queen's Colleges."[177]

Gladstone would not be thanked for his efforts. In England he would be overthrown as German liberalism was overthrown by Bismarck, while in Ireland a party was founded to make even greater demands: Home Rule. A County by-election was made necessary in 1872 by the succession of Lord Kenmare's son to the earldom and to the House of Lords. Home Rule decided to run a candidate in the person of young Rowland Ponsonby Blennerhassett of Kells. For years the two Killarney houses of Herbert and Kenmare had swapped the representation by agreement. Both were pro-Catholic and had Bishop Moriarty's support. Now this agreement was rendered almost futile by the nomination of a Home Ruler. The Bishop's opposition to Fenianism was well known, and if Home Rule was a constitutional alternative to Fenianism, it was a constitutionalism heavily tinged with physical action, many of the erstwhile Fenians having joined the new movement. Tralee took enthusiastically to Home Rule and many of the priests prepared to defy their unionist Bishop. There was fresh provocation in the manner in which Lord Ventry's freeholders were drilled into formation by Lord Ventry's brother, Captain Mullins of the Kerry Militia, and marched to Tralee to cast their vote. This was the last "open vote" election, when voters had to declare openly their intended choice; in future elections Dean Mawe's dream of a secret ballot would be realised. Patrick Foley, writing a little over thirty years later, describes what happened on the journey to Tralee for the poll of 9 February. Before ever they reached the town they received an extremely hostile reception:

"Fearing obstruction or the placing of explosives along Connor Hill Mountain Pass, the route was reconnoitred several times by cavalry, and excessive precautions taken to guard against a plot. On their way to Connor Hill, some of the horse guides cut the tackling, and having hidden the drafting chains, pretended they were maliciously damaged or stolen."

Near Castlegregory "the passage was blocked by obstructions being placed across the road". The commanding officer, sensing that the voters considered themselves captives, and feeling uneasy under military protection, protested to Captain Mullins that his men were doing the work of bailiffs. Fr O'Kane, PP Castlegregory, now saw his chance to intervene:

"Ah, you sons of Kerry, where is your pride and manhood to be dragged like prisoners or carted like cattle in this way? And for what? That you may give a stab to your country – Poor Ireland."

The words of the priest did it: "many now jumped from the carts. The military escort, having marched away from the scene, every man, woman and child immediately fell upon the Dingle contingent, beating them with seaweed *foums*, this quickly compelling them to retreat to their own homes by glens, valleys and mountains."[178] The Home Rule candidate, Blennerhassett, won the election, defeating the candidate of Lords Ventry and Kenmare – and Bishop Moriarty. The priests, at least Fr Kane, had their way despite the Bishop. In the end, according to the *Times*, the police succeeded in bringing only 13 of the Ventry voters into Tralee, out of the 180 who left Castlegregory.[179]

Home Rule rallied public opinion, including the priests, well before the general election to come. In 1870 the Parish Priest of Ardfert, Fr O'Donoghue sued Sam Hussey for libel after remarks of Hussey about him in the *Cork Examiner* (though the report of the case neglected to advise that he had called Sam Hussey "the Uriah Heep among Kerry landlords").[180] The priests were usually on the side of the people during the campaign, but there was a significant change when an outrage was perpetrated against one of their parishioners, perhaps a shooting for the payment of rent when payment was forbidden by the local branch of the League.

The O'Donoghue had changed his politics to oppose Home Rule by the run up to the election of 1874. His opponents claimed that he had betrayed the electorate. He barely defeated the Home Rule candidate John Daly (143 to 140). The Home Rulers are clearly the radical street politicians in Tralee at this time, but the influence of the Liberal unionists of Kerry, including Bishop Moriarty, helped delay for a number of years their coming of age as the dominant force in Irish politics. The O'Donoghue espoused Gladstone's policies rather than Home Rule, beginning with the Disestablishment of the Church of Ireland, for which, together with the Land Act of 1870 and reform of the jury system, he said the people should be grateful. But he was declared a bankrupt in 1870 and then the rumour went around that Gladstone had offered him a job. The Home Rulers, fresh from having foiled the Ventry voters, provided a very hostile reception for The O'Donoghue when he arrived from Killarney by train and tried to address the crowd in front of Benners Hotel.[181] Such was O'Donoghue's unpopularity that he might easily have been defeated in Tralee. Sam Hussey and the unionists remained aloof fearing that if they put up a candidate they would only hand a victory to the Home Rulers. No doubt they were also grateful for the Bishop's instructions to his clergy to remain out of the contest.

The 1874 general election put Gladstone out of power and brought back the Conservatives under Disraeli. But the election brought a sweeping victory for Home Rule, at the same time sounding the death knell of liberal unionism as a political force. The era of Bishop Moriarty was at an end; a new era had begun, one identified with a radical parliamentary leader named Charles Stewart Parnell, with whom the issue of the farms would return to the centre of Irish politics.

Sam Hussey

Tralee: The Public Market (The Wrench Series No. 9543, postmark appears Sep 16, 1904).
In 1847 a new market place to the north of the Mall was opened. The lighting, cleansing and watching of the town were provided for by legislation and paid for out of the rate struck by the Town Commissioners, though the burden of the county cess, levied by the Grand Jury, also weighed on the shoulders of the townspeople.

[132] N.A.I., State Paper 1835/31; Tralee, 27 February 1817.

[133] *D.J.*, 30 August 1817

[134] *L.C.*, Wednesday 8 May, August 21, 22 1822, report from Tralee; see also the *Dublin Evening Post*, 26 October 1822.

[135] M. MacSweeney, "Blennerville 1088-1853 – the Shifting Fortunes of a Kerry Village", *J.K.A.H.S.*, 2003, pp.125-147, p.130.

[136] *L.C.*, 19 April 1826; *Limerick Gazette*, 30 June, 1820 "Mr. William John Neligan of Tralee" is "receiver of the rents &c of the extensive estate of Sir Edward Denny".

[137] Reproduced in the *K. E. P.*, 13 November 1915; information from Sir Anthony Denny on the re-use of the stone fragments, quoting his father, historian Rev. Sir Henry Lyttelton Lyster Denny.

[138] *K.E.P* 20 Nov. 1915, quoting a contemporary Dublin publication.

[139] Annie Rowan, *K.E.P.*, 30 Nov. 1895.

[140] *L.C.*, 7, 24 July 1824.

[141] Ibid. 8 September 1824 (Tralee Sept. 4); the edition of 15 September (Tralee 11 September) 1825 celebrates "the progress made in the Butter Trade, since the establishment of a Weigh-House (which has) far exceeded our most sanguine expectations. The amount of the carriage to Cork is no longer deducted in this market by the butter buyers from the farmers".

[142] *L.C.*, 15 September 1825.

[143] *Limerick General Advertiser*, 4 (14?) April 1820, Buckley execution; *L.C.*, 26 April 1826, Lovett execution.

[144] *L.C., 14 August 1824*

[145] John J. O Riordain, *Where Araglen So Gently Flows*, 2007, pp.162-169.

[146] *Endowed Schools, Ireland, Commission* (Dublin 1857); The Commission, sitting in Tralee in 1855, heard that the school on Strand Street suffered a great reduction in numbers on account of "the general depression throughout the country, emigration and other causes".

[147] N.A.I., S.O.C. 431/2295/22 Francis Drew, Meanus, to Charles Grant, November 25th 1821.

[148] *F. J.*, 5 July 1826; *L.C.*, 5 July 1826; *K.E.P.*, 29 August 1914.

[149] R.I.A. Day Papers, 12w16, diary entry of Judge Day, 8 August 1828.

[150] *London Times*, 17 September 1828.

[151] The *Western Herald*, June 29, 1829. It is tempting to consider that the Tralee democrats may have heard about the scenes in Washington following the inauguration of Andrew Jackson earlier in 1829 when the White House was invaded by the over-enthusiastic supporters of the new President.

[152] Wellington Papers, WP1/1239/10, Hartley Library, University of Southampton, Maurice Fitzgerald to Arthur Wellesley (the Duke of Wellington), 6 December 1832.

[153] *L.C.*, 1, 5, 19 December 1832. Maurice O'Connell held the Tralee representation in 1832-7 and again in 1838-53, to be succeeded by his brother Daniel, youngest son of *The Liberator*, in the years 1853-63.

[154] British Parliamentary Papers, vol. xxvii, *Local Government in Southern Ireland* 1835.

[155] *L.C.*, 9 August 1837.

[156] *L.C.*, 16 August 1837.

[157] Archdeacon Arthur Blennerhassett Rowan, *A Plea from the Protestants of Ireland, to the Right Hon. Lord Morpeth, Chief Secretary for Ireland*, Dublin 1840.

[158] Annie Rowan, *Kerry Evening Post*, 5 October 1895.

[159] Bob FitzSimons, "Medicine and Society in Nineteenth-Century Kerry", *J. K.A.H.S.* 1994, pp. 7, 15, 53.

[160] *L.C.* 15 August 1832. Dr Mawe's sister and niece are reported dead of the contagion in the same week as Dr Mawe.

[161] R.I.A., Day Ms. 12w17; Judge Day, Loughlinstown, 5 May 1833.

[162] Russell McMorran, "Archdeacon Rowan, founder of *The Kerry Magazine*", in the *Kerry Magazine*, 1989.

[163] Rev. A. B. Rowan, *Romanism in the Church, illustrated by the case of E.G. Browne as stated in the letters of the Rev. Dr. Pusey*, Belmont 1847.

[164] Shane G. Lehane, *The Great Famine in the Poor Law Unions of Dingle and Killarney, Co. Kerry, 1845-52* (M.A. thesis National University of Ireland, U.C.C. 2005), p.114.

[165] McMorran, "Rowan, The Kerry Magazine", p.5.

[166] Christine Kinealy, *The Great Calamity, The Irish Famine 1845-52*, 1994.

[167] The sons of the absentee third Baronet resident in Tralee are Rev. Anthony Denny, Rector of Tralee, his brother Rev. Henry Denny, Vicar of Churchill, Clogherbrien and Annagh, and William Denny, estate agent and election activist.

[168] *Dublin Magazine*, February 1834, reproduced in *Kerry Evening Post* 17 November 1915.

[169] *The Tralee Chronicle* report in *The Munster News and Provincial Advertiser*, 23 June 1852.

[170] Ibid.

[171] *M.N.*, 17 July 1852.

[172] Quoted in Theodore Hoppen, *Elections, Politics and Society in Ireland 1833-1855*, edn. 1984. p. 78.

[173] Endowed Schools Commission, 2 vols, 1857 (Tralee evidence of 1855).

[174] At the funeral of Charles Kickham in 1882 the administrator in the cathedral in Thurles refused to admit the coffin to the church. Archbishop Croke later assured the family that had he been in Ireland he would have acted otherwise; R. V. Comerford, *Charles J. Kickham*, Dublin 1979, p. 174.

[175] *I.T.*, 15, 18 May 1863.

[176] R.V. Comerford, *The Fenians in Context, Irish Politics and Society 1848-82* (1985), p. 57; R. McMorran, "The Mount Hawk Races", *The Kerry Magazine* 2005.

[177] Mary Hickson, *Kerry Evening Post* of 24 July 1880; she had converted to Catholicism briefly during the 1860s. It is by no means certain that she was opposed to Home Rule.

[178] Patrick Foley, *History of the County Kerry, Corkaguiny*, Dublin 1907, pp. 241-252.

[179] *I.T.*, 10 February 1872.

[180] Sam Hussey, *Reminiscences of an Irish Land Agent* (London 1904) p. 96, 97; *I.T.*, 23 March 1870.

[181] *I.T.*, 11 September 1873; 3 February 1874 for O'Donoghue's manifesto to the Tralee electorate.

SEVEN

INDEPENDENCE

1. THE 1880S, THE LAND LEAGUERS TAKE OVER THE TRALEE POOR LAW UNION: GLADSTONE INTRODUCES ANOTHER LAND ACT

By the time of Gladstone's return to power in 1880, an accumulation of grievances weighed heavily on the shoulders of Tralee's unionists. It was Gladstone who had disestablished the Church of Ireland and introduced the first of his Land Acts. Sam Hussey hated the Gladstone programme, believing that Kerry had enjoyed relative peace for fifty years until Gladstone capitulated to the power of the priests. The then Marquess of Lansdowne, an appointee of Gladstone at the Foreign Office, declined to serve the Prime Minister and parted company with his administration. For the 1880 general election there would be no keeping the unionists out of the Tralee contest; Sam Hussey offered himself for election against The O'Donoghue, who had meanwhile returned to the Home Rule fold. Hussey could claim greater residency credentials, living as he did at Edenburn. Hussey was defeated, and he blamed the priests, complaining that "man proposes and priest disposes".[182] It was the last election before the Tralee constituency was abolished.

1879 brought a renewal of famine conditions throughout the west of Ireland, and with it a spate of evictions. Michael Davitt founded the Land League, drawing on his own experience of being evicted with his family when a child from their Mayo farm. The land war in Kerry began in the latter half of 1880. By then there was a successor to Isaac Butt at the head of Home Rule. This was the charismatic figure of Charles Stewart Parnell. He brokered an arrangement with Michael Davitt and the American Fenian John Devoy to merge the activities of Home Rule, the surviving Fenian spirit – and the Land League. It became known as the New Departure. Parnell urged the ostracisation of land grabbers. He also urged the League to challenge for control of the boards of guardians in the Poor Law unions, and Tralee, having taken Parnell at his word, earned the most spectacular League victory in the country-wide Poor Law elections of March 1881. Key to the success was Timothy Harrington, ably assisted by his brother Edward, and Timothy's newspaper the *Kerry Sentinel*. The Harringtons, natives of Berehaven in Co. Cork, had come to Tralee about four years earlier to work as teachers. With the Poor Law election in his sights, Timothy organised a number of meetings in the Tralee union, at which it was made very clear to voters what the League expected of them. Then he published the resolution in his newspaper. The result was that the League won two of the four seats in the Tralee division where heretofore they had none. The scene was now set for the removal of the Chairman, the popular figure of William Rowan (son of Archdeacon Arthur Blennerhassett Rowan), and Rowan was duly removed, though not at the first attempt.[183]

The first of Gladstone's land acts had been of little use because, though it tried to reward evicted tennants for improvements made, in the end it alienating the landlords as well as the tenants. Gladstone's second attempt, the Land Bill of 1881, did little to pacify Kerry, or Ireland generally, and when Charles Stewart Parnell rejected its terms he was thrown in jail. He was released in early 1882 as part of a deal to pacify the country. Then the country was shocked by the murder in the Phoenix Park of the new Irish Chief Secretary who had arrived in the country that very morning.

The district of Tralee was not to be pacified. A land agent named Arthur Herbert was shot dead near Castleisland on 30 March 1882, while walking home to Killeentierna where he lived with his mother. He had attended the Castleisland Petty Sessions. Usually he drove in a mail phaeton, but that day he walked. The government offered a reward of £500 for information leading to the arrest and prosecution of the killers, and £3000 for information leading to a conviction.[184] Herbert worked as agent to a Mr Hartnett, and when rents were withheld he personally attended the eviction of a tenant. After an occasion of rioting he declared that an appropriate response would be to "skiver the people", adding that "if he were present he should have used buckshot".[185]

Six months after the murder of Arthur Herbert, Castleisland was again in the daily news. The *Times* of 7 October 1882 announced "another murder near Castleisland", that of Thomas Browne, described as "a comfortable farmer". Archdeacon O'Connell denounced the murder at Mass in Scartaglin, saying that "ideas most perverse had taken hold of the hearts of the people". Shortly afterwards, charges were preferred against Silvester Poff and James Barrett.[186] The testimony of the principal witness, Ellen Brosnan, placed both men in the field where the body of Thomas Browne was found. Both were convicted and sentenced to be hanged. There was widespread revulsion at the proceedings and at the prospect of the executions. The London *Times* carried a report that the Tralee Board of Guardians had sent a petition to the government to pardon Sylvester Poff and James Barrett, the petition stating that "a strong feeling exists in the locality that the condemned prisoners were not the perpetrators of the crime"; when the executioner, Marwood, arrived in Tralee, no local carpenter would assist him in erecting a scaffold, so a team of carpenters was brought in from Dublin.[187] Historian Mary Agnes Hickson was less concerned with finding the true killers than with connecting the killings of Herbert and farmer Browne with the activities of Tim Harrington. Poff and Barrett were merely "ignorant misguided" cottiers, "while he (Tim Harrington) was deliberately trading in agitation to enter parliament":

"Timothy Harrington is the worst of the whole set. I knew him ... ten years ago when he first established his newspaper in Tralee under the patronage of the Dominican Monks. I used to write sometimes in it the Kerry history and antiquities &c but latterly especially after two Kerry cottiers Poff and Barrett were hung for a murder at Castle Island and after Arthur Herbert was murdered there I never spoke to Mr Harrington, being morally convinced that his inflammatory speeches and writings in his paper had brought about those crimes[188]

Herbert's "buckshot" remark had been eagerly printed in the *Kerry Sentinel*, and condemned in the House of Commons by Irish MPs, including Mr Healy. The Irish Lord Chancellor had asked Herbert for an explanation, and when Herbert gave it the Chancellor proposed to proceed no further. But a round robin was posted up around Castleisland containing a condemnation of Herbert.

2. TRALEE PART OF THE NEW WEST KERRY CONSTITUENCY AND THE PLAN OF CAMPAIGN

Tim Harrington handed over the running of the *Kerry Sentinel* to his brother Edward Harrington when he departed for Dublin to become secretary to the National League. A government crackdown on those involved in the rural campaign was made possible by a Prevention of Crime Act passed in the wake of the Phoenix Park murders. Edward Harrington was prosecuted in 1883 and endured his first imprisonment for publishing a seditious notice in the *Sentinel*.

The Conservatives achieved power in 1885 under Prime Minister Lord Salisbury, who, with nephew Balfour, the Irish Chief Secretary, was committed to a course of repression in Ireland. The rural campaign was already in full swing in Kerry by the time Salisbury came to power. Meanwhile, the Moonlighters were the latest representatives of the rural campaign in the south of Ireland. At the end of 1884 they dynamited Sam Hussey's home at Edenburn, half way between Tralee and Castleisland; and the County Club and the Court House were given round the clock police protection. It may be that Hussey gained his nickname "The Woodcock" at this period, for being shot at many times and surviving.

Hussey became one of the principal targets of the Plan of Campaign, which was the new strategy of the National League. Under the Plan the tenants would offer a reduced rent to the landlord, and if this was rejected the money would be deposited in the bank to be used to help the tenants after eviction. Edward Harrington and his brother Tim became centrally involved in the National League and the Plan of Campaign in Kerry. Edward attended a public meeting on Sunday the 3rd of May, 1885 in front of the Temperance Hall in Dingle to help establish a branch of the Irish National League, which led to the introduction of emergency men, which in turn provoked the National League to order boycotting. When Atkins's shop continued to serve the emergency men the shop was boycotted. The killings at Castle Farm, near Molahiffe Castle, Firies, six months later were blamed on agents of the Conservative government of Lord Salisbury as a strike against the power of the National League in Kerry. John Curtin of Castle Farm was a prominent member of the local National League, he had recently paid a subscription to the eviction fund, and had taken part in a delegation to Lord Kenmare seeking a rent reduction. Aged in his early sixties, he and his family put up a fierce struggle to deny their assailants the guns they had come to take, shooting dead one of them before John Curtin himself was shot and killed. When Fr Murphy, from the altar of the chapel at Farranfore, denounced the Moonlighters for the murder of John Curtin, part of the congregation walked out in protest. In October, shortly before the killings at Castle Farm, the latest residence of Sam Hussey was attacked; this was Aghadoe House which Hussey had rented from Lord Headley. Within days of the murder at Castle Farm, Edward Harrington was nominated to stand for one of the Kerry constituencies in the newly drawn electoral carve-up of Kerry: he stood for West Kerry, which included Tralee. He was nominated on 24 November 1885 at the Court House, Tralee, and in the ensuing election he defeated William Rowan.[189]

1885 and 1886 were years dominated by the activities of the Moonlighters. So serious was the situation in Kerry in 1886 that the government appointed a military hero, Sir Redvers Buller, as special commissioner over the Royal Irish Constabulary. Buller made quite an impression by appearing in Killarney and Tralee without the usual security detail. In Tralee he was entertained to lunch at the County Club and he met Sam Hussey at Hussey's Denny Street office.

In 1887 there were wholesale evictions on the estate of Lord Cork at Ballyferriter; in response, the Plan of Campaign was implemented, and Patrick Ferriter, one of the leaders, was prosecuted in Dingle. By this time Mary Agnes Hickson had departed Tralee for her home in retirement, 30 Kingston College, Mitchelstown. (She had tried to obtain employment under the Historic Manuscripts Commission, without success.) Without knowing it she was moving to one of the most dangerous towns in Ireland – and Tim Harrington would be among those who came to Mitchelstown to stoke the fires of agitation for the Plan of Campaign. The riots in Mitchelstown in 1887 were relayed around the world as a result of a happy coincidence, a telegraph machine available for use in the town, and the chance presence of an international journalist. The League marched its farmers into the town in impressive array, and were joined by the recently formed Gaelic Athletic Association – and, of course, the priests. Prominent organisers of the Kingston tenantry at Mitchelstown included William O'Brien, MP for Mallow, and John Mandeville, chairman of the Mitchelstown board of guardians. The heavy-handed response of the police to the riot was believed to have government sanction, in particular that of Chief Secretary Arthur Balfour who earned the nickname "Bloody Balfour" because of the conduct of the police at Mitchelstown. Mary Hickson was then in correspondence with her colleague historian William Hartpole Lecky, at this time completing his *History of England*. She had this to say about Balfour's police:

> "The police officers and magistrates here certainly acted rather unwisely in waiting to send sixteen policemen through a dense crowd of several thousand Irish farmers and cottiers, many of them on horseback."

But Harrington and the Plan of Campaign were at the root of the problem: "Lady Kingston has last week made a fair offer to her tenants, but Harrington and the rest of his set will not allow them to accept it".[190]

Despite the support given the Plan by Archbishop Croke of Cashel, the Pope issued a rescript in 1888 in which he condemned it. In that year Mandeville endured many privations at the hands of the prison system in Tullamore and died as a consequence. His statue stands in the Square in Mitchelstown. Edward Harrington followed Mandeville to Tullamore Jail. First he served a term in the Jail in Tralee. Did Mary Hickson, at Mitchelstown, read the *Irish Times* of 7 January 1888, where it was stated that Harrington was released, "having completed the term of one month's imprisonment ... for publishing reports of meetings of suppressed branches of the National League in his paper, the *Kerry Sentinel*"?[191] Later, in December of the same year, he was re-arrested and sentenced to a further spell in prison, this time in Tullamore, where he was subjected to the stages of systematic humiliation experienced by Mandeville before him, including solitary confinement, removal of books, food deprivation and enforced wearing of prison clothes. Sympathetic propaganda put it about that Harrington was *Mandevilled*. (John Mendeville had died on 8 July 1888.)[192]

One of those movements that participated in the Mitchelstown protest was the recently formed Gaelic Athletic Association. It had organised in Kerry in 1885 with a meeting in Tralee. Edward Harrington refused to give the new movement the support of the Irish National League, so the GAA enthusiasts removed Harrington from the presidency of the League in Kerry. Part of Harrington's difficulty with the GAA stemmed from his involvement with a predecessor organisation for athletics in the county (the GAA organised more than just football and hurling). But there seems to have been another difficulty: Harrington was a Home Ruler, whilst his opponents, notably Moore Stack, were of the Fenian tradition. Archbishop Croke of Cashel, the patron of the GAA, tried to stay out of the Kerry dispute. Croke knew Tralee well: his grandmother owned a shop at the corner of the Mall and the Square, and he came there often as a boy; according to his biographer, he retained a slight Kerry accent all his life. The GAA came to own the sports ground of their rivals, renaming it Austin Stack Park after Moore Stack's son, a republican and one of the county's early football heroes.

3. TRALEE IN THE 1890S:
THE GAELIC LEAGUE A UNIFYING CAUSE

For many, the transformation in the rural areas consequent on the Land Acts ushered in the *real* Irish revolution, which, for its tangible lasting effect on the countryside and villages and towns, surpassed the political and cultural changes to be considered in the next chapter.

Tomb at Powick of Sir Edward Denny 3rd Bart. and wife Elizabeth Day.
Photograph Terry Maple

The Blennerhassett estate was declared insolvent by the Court of Chancery in 1885 and taken into the custody of the Court, finally sold to the tenants under the terms of the Land Acts, the Blennerhassett family retaining custody of Ballyseedy and the surrounding demesne.[193] Sir Edward Denny, fourth Baronet, the *hymn maker*, lived to over ninety years of age, dying in 1889. He never married. His younger brother, Robert Day Denny (b.1800) predeceased him and so never inherited the estate; but the latter's son, Robert Arthur Denny, became the fifth Baronet. When Robert Arthur inherited, he was deeply in debt, having spent lavishly in the expectation that his father would inherit the estate and clear his debts. When his father died and his creditors pounced, Robert Arthur was forced to make an expensive settlement. On succeeding his uncle Sir Edward in 1889, he was still £200,000 in debt. The Tralee portion of the estate was sold off in 1891: the purchaser was Dr Clemente Finnarty, the price £40,000. The remainder of the estate was sold in June 1899 – practically all that remained of the "Seignory of Denny-vale after it had been 312 years in the family".[194]

The Home Rule movement was in disarray from 1891 after the campaign to remove Parnell, and Parnell's death. Parnell's great personal mystique was shattered by the divorce proceedings of one of his party's MPs, Captain Willie O'Shea. O'Shea's wife, Katherine, was Parnell's lover, and the intimate details of Katherine's and Parnell's relationship were published in the newspapers, with no opportunity given Parnell to put his side. Victorian Britain and Ireland were shocked. Gladstone told the Irish party that his leadership of the Liberals would be meaningless if Parnell stayed, and priests throughout Kerry subscribed to a resolution demanding Parnell's removal. The subsequent generations never forgave those who drove Parnell on his last desperate campaign to shore up support for his leadership; the high-minded William Butler Yeats, poet and Nobel laureate, blamed it all on the influence of O'Connell whose tactics in conflict, he believed, had coarsened Irish public life.

A number of years pass before the Home Rule factions re-unite under John Redmond, and by then the initiative is taken, not by Home Rule, but by a new movement with a new radical agenda: Sinn Féin. If the decade of the 1890s threatened disillusion, new life was breathed into Irish nationalism from a surprising source. In 1892 Douglas Hyde delivered an address to the National Literary Society entitled *The Necessity for De-Anglicising Ireland*. In the following year the Gaelic League (Conradh na Gaeilge), was founded to keep alive the Irish language and Irish culture. A contemporary and world famous Irish Literary Revival was sympathetic to the aims of Hyde; its exponents, chief among whom were John Millington Synge and William Butler Yeats, wrote in English. Synge visited the Great Blasket, and in 1907 his *Playboy of the Western World*, featuring a Kerryman who decamps to Mayo having killed his father, was staged at the Abbey Theatre. The Irish Literary Theatre (which became the Abbey Theatre, and then the National Theatre of Ireland) provided the forum for shared activity. Douglas Hyde, an academic and linguist, wrote plays in for the Abbey Theatre, as did Yeats and Synge. Son of a Protestant clergyman from Roscommon, Hyde learned the Irish language from the servants at his father's rectory. Even Mary Hickson was not unaffected by the cultural revival: when she wrote from her address at 3 Church Street, Tralee in 1884 to apply for work with the Historic Manuscripts Commission she offered references from, among others, Samuel Ferguson who inspired the poet Yeats and others associated with the Irish Literary Revival.[195] Her other referees included Kerry-connected members of the Historic Manuscripts Commission: Lord Edmond FitzMaurice (1846-1935), of the Lansdowne family, and Charles Graves, later Protestant Bishop of Limerick (the diocese to which Kerry belongs). Graves had deep roots in Kerry[196] and was a friend of Archdeacon Rowan, of Belmont; though Rowan died in 1861,

Graves and his family continued to come to a summer home at Parknasilla. Rowan had introduced Graves to local antiquarian Richard Hitchcock, of Annagh, west of Tralee, and through his work with Hitchcock Graves became a leading expert on the Ogham stones of West Kerry. Graves died in 1899 the same year as Mary Hickson.

Mary Hickson's family was from Hillville, near where the road ascends to the Connor Pass on the way to Dingle. Her father, John James Hickson, was a lawyer and legal estate agent. When the family fell on hard times after the Famine, they moved to Tralee where his father-in-law (Rev. James Day) had been Rector in Napoleonic times. John James inspired his daughter's love of history: "when I walked or rode with him and a brother about my own age, getting … field lessons in history in and around Tralee, and in Corcaguiny."[197] John James died young leaving Mary Hickson's mother unprovided and his daughter in straightened circumstances all her life. Now her achievement seems extraordinary. With few precedents, apart from Charles Smith's and the Nun of Kenmare's *Historys* of Kerry, in 1756 and 1871 respectively, she produced her invaluable *Old Kerry Records*, series one and two in 1872 and 1874.[198]

4. THE TWENTIETH CENTURY, THE EASTER REBELLION OF 1916

The Local Government Act of 1898 abolished the old Town Commission and the Grand Jury, and substituted new Urban and County Councils. About then, the railings at the end of Denny Street were removed, permitting access to what is now the Town Park, the former Bowling Green of Letitia Coningsby. A committee had been at work for some time to commemorate the centenary of the Rebellion of 1798. Its planned statue of the Pikeman failed to meet the deadline. Then in 1902 Maud Gonne McBride laid the foundation stone for the Pikeman. She was the subject of many poems by Yeats, and her husband had fought in the Boer War.

With the dawning of the new century the page was turned on the series of failed Irish rebellions of the century past. Britain's Empire was rocked by the Boer War, and domestically by events like the trial of writer Oscar Wilde, whose mother, Speranza had written for *The Nation*. Yet there seemed no immediate danger to the union of Ireland and Britain. The Home Rule party was re-united and it was believed that the concession of home rule would seal the Union. A Home Rule bill was actually passed at Westminster in 1912 and it would come into force in two years. Then it was postponed when the First World War broke out. It was a fatal postponement as the initiative was now handed to the republican movement which saw Britain's difficulty as Ireland's opportunity.

In the early years of the new century the Blasket Islands (formerly Ferriter's Islands) were home to a pre-industrial population that spoke only Irish and had as yet little experience of emigration. This would change with the advent of tourism; the girls would leave the island to enter paid employment, and the boys and young men would follow them. The earliest of the tourists were scholars. Tralee was the gateway to the West for Gaelic scholars arriving by train from Dublin, where they rested a while before heading west on the narrow gauge railway to Dingle. They included leading academics – some from European institutes – as well as students, and future leaders of the national struggle. Carl Marstrander, a Norwegian linguist, came to the Great Blasket where he was taught by Tomás Ó Criomhthain, who also taught Robin Flower, Yorkshireman and Deputy Keeper of Manuscripts at the British Museum. Marstrander and Flower came in 1907 and 1910 respectively. Others followed, including future politicians such as Ernán de Blaghd who spent a summer holiday in Kinard in 1913 at the home of the Ashes.[199] Thomas Ashe and fellow Kerryman *The* O'Rahilly were among those in the Irish Republican Brotherhood who tightened their grip on the Gaelic League at this time, and this precipitated the resignation of the League's President, Douglas Hyde, when the League decided in 1915 to become politicised. Many believe that the Gaelic League filled the ranks of the Volunteers, but it was the Irish Republican Brotherhood (I.R.B), operating from within the Irish Volunteers, that would stage the Easter Rebellion of 1916.

Volunteer companies were raised at the beginning of the Great War. The first of them was in Ulster. Dublin followed. The ostensible purpose of the Volunteers was to defend Ireland against a German invasion; but John Redmond offered them as recruits to the British army. On 13 October 1914, Kerry's Volunteers met at the Rink in Tralee. There was a heated debate on the question of recruitment. Tom O'Donnell, MP West Kerry (which included Tralee), was a great recruiter; he was not a Volunteer, so he was asked to leave the meeting and the meeting voted heavily against recruitment.

Dublin was the principal venue of the 1916 insurrection, but there was an important, failed prequel at Banna Strand, near Tralee. Sir Roger Casement was put ashore from a submarine on Good Friday to await the gun cargo of a German vessel named the Aud. Not having eaten properly for days, and in an exhausted condition, he was arrested next morning and brought to Tralee where he was detained in the R.I.C. barracks before being transferred to Dublin and thence to London. He was later hanged for treason. He could easily have been rescued in Tralee: the door of the police barracks was left open by a sympathetic head constable, John Kearney. Against the background of this failure in Kerry the Easter Rising took place on Easter Monday. The Rising was suppressed over the course of a week with much destruction to Dublin – and then Britain made the fatal mistake of executing the leaders by firing squad.

Thomas Ashe

Thomas Ashe survived the bloodshed of Easter Week and the firing squad, but he became Kerry's great martyr in the cause of Irish independence. He was born in 1885 as the Plan of Campaign began, later moving to Dublin to train as a primary teacher, teaching at Lusk in north Co. Dublin. As a native Irish speaker, and possessed of a warm and engaging personality, he threw himself into Gaelic activities, founding a piper's club and participating in *feiseanna*. He organised the Volunteers in North Dublin and led the attack on the police barracks at Ashbourne. Having spent time in prison after the Rising, he was rearrested in 1917 and went on hunger strike. In his final captivity he was subjected to the food deprivation and other indignities suffered by Edward Harrington and John Mandeville, but with the addition of the forced feeding from which he died. A fund-raising began for the construction of the Ashe Memorial Hall in the months after Ashe's death.

Kerry has never quite come to terms with the failure to rescue Sir Roger Casement. The argument of "what might have been" if the West of Ireland had risen to support the Rising in Dublin has gone on for three generations, and we know today about the high numbers of Volunteerss throughout Kerry who were on standby for the call to rise. Ashe, had he lived, might have become president of Sinn Féin in 1917, and then there might have been no Civil War.[200] With the death of Ashe, Eamon De Valera was the only surviving commandant of the 1916 Rising. In October 1917, De Valera was elected president of Sinn Féin, the organisation that unified the various revolutionary groupings. Next, Britain introduced conscription, and this proved a godsend to Sinn Féin in the 1918 general election in which the party swept the country and virtually removed Home Rule from Irish politics. The War of Independence began early in 1919, to be followed by Ireland's Civil War after the peace proposals were accepted by some and rejected by the party of De Valera: Ireland was to lose Ulster, which would remain under Britain, and the rest of the island would gain independence but continue in the British Commonwealth.

5. WAR OF INDEPENDENCE AND CIVIL WAR

The supposed quiet of Kerry during the War of Independence (now being revisited by the historians) is to be measured against the exceptional activity of Tom Barry at the head of his Brigade in West Cork. (Barry had entered the British Army while still a boy and served in Mesopotamia.) One incident may be cited to overturn the received wisdom about Kerry.[201] On the night of 31 October 1920 thirteen policemen were shot and two others were kidnapped. In reprisal the Black and Tans laid siege to Tralee for the next nine days. There was enormous international publicity. *Le Journal de Paris* printed a report from a visitor to Tralee at the time, stating that Tralee was more terrorised than any town he had seen in France during the First World War. "The town was as deserted and doleful as if the Angel of Death has passed through it", he wrote. "Not a living soul in the streets. All the shops shut and the bolts hastily fastened. All work was suspended."

It is not proposed here to go down the highways and byways of the Civil War that followed the War of Independence which ended with the severance of the six northeastern counties from the partly-independent Free State. The scars of the short but brutal Civil War would last for generations and memory was suppressed in an effort to come to terms with the horrors perpetrated by Republicans and their opponents, the army of the new Free State. When I grew up in Tralee during the 1950s and 1960s our parents told us nothing of the Massacre at Ballyseedy when nine Republicans were taken by Free Staters from Ballymullen Barracks, tied to a mine at Ballyseedy and blown up. The GAA helped heal the wounds of civil war when a number of leading soldiers on both sides became friends on the field of play. The role of the GAA in this regard can never be overstated when we reflect on a typical attendance figure of perhaps 20,000 at a club game in Austin Stack Park on Friday evenings during the 1930s. When Con Brosnan became a famous Kerry footballer, he played with Republicans like John Joe Sheehy and Joe Barrett. In 1924, the year after the Civil War ended, Brosnan arranged a safe conduct for Sheehy to play in the All Ireland final held in the Gaelic Grounds in Limerick. In a matching gesture, when Tralee man Joe Barrett was selected to captain a later Kerry team, he gave up the honour and passed it to Con Brosnan.

Kevin O'Higgins, a minister in the first Free State government, stated that ours was the most conservative revolution in the world. In truth the social revolution had already taken place when the farmers received their farms from the landlords under the Land Acts. The 1930s brought the government of Mr De Valera. He deepened the effects of the international recession, caused by the Wall Street Crash, by starting the Economic War with England after he refused to pass on to England the annuities agreed for the transfer of the farms. The platform at Tralee railway station was filled with emigrants. Poor young men and girls from Cromane and Callinafersy stood outside St John's to hire themselves to the big farmers of North Kerry. In the midst of poverty there was some innovation, like the new housing estates built in the late 1930s to relocate residents of the old lanes: John Mitchel's, Stack's and O Rahilly's Villas; after World War II came Kevin Barry Villas, St Brendan's Park, Casement's Avenue, and Marian and St John's Park.

Charlie Kerins

De Valera released the IRA prisoners when he came to power, but there was no peace dividend, only a new IRA campaign: the Bombing Campaign of 1939 brought IRA activity to mainland England, then to the Six Counties of Northern Ireland, finally to the southern State. Charlie Kerins of Caherina, Tralee, was charged with the killing of detective Sergeant Denis

O'Brien, a member of the *Broy Harriers*, a group within the new police considered by the IRA too diligent in the pursuit of their members. Kerins, a former scholarship boy and footballer, had risen up the ranks quickly and was believed to be the IRA Deputy Chief of Staff. Sergeant Denis O'Brien was killed at his home in Ballyboden, Dublin as he drove in his car down his driveway. Charlie Kerins was later arrested in Rathmines and an arsenal of weapons was found in his room. He was tried before a military tribunal under the emergency legislation; there were no witnesses and no jury. He refused to recognise the court and was found guilty. The day before his execution Kerry TD Dan Spring told the Dail that the trial and conviction were giving rise to serious concerns and that there should be a stay of execution. De Valera held tough and Spring was ordered out of the Dail when he persisted. Another deputy, Oliver J. Flanagan, from one of the Midland constituencies, was equally vociferous in the cause of Kerins, to no avail. The hanging took place on 1 December 1944; Albert Pierrepoint, the English hangman, was brought over to do the work. Aspects of the trial and conviction of Charlie Kerins have troubled Tralee and Kerry ever since. The evidence used against him, some finger prints on a bicycle said to be his, the nature of the tribunal, De Valera's campaign against his old comrades in arms, the use of Albert Pierrepoint, finally Charlie Kerins's own character – all these have ensured that Tralee has never forgotten Charlie Kerins.

Hard times continued in the 1950s. Gil Brien's band, heard regularly in the town on public occasions, manifested a spirit of local and national pride. Revington's drapery, whose Edwardian façade continues to dominate the Mall, was the largest shop in town. The flour mills of McCowans and Latchfords, important relics of the second half of the nineteenth century, covered a large area in Edward Street. When a pencil or a jotter cost a penny, some students in primary school found it hard to pay. St Joseph's Monastery School was home to orphaned boys whom we saw regularly when the school band played on public occasions, never suspecting that the 1990s would reveal a darker side of life in such institutions. My generation was the first to avail of free secondary education. That was in 1964.

Horse doctors, cow doctors, charmers and ethno vets held sway
in rural areas even after the advent of town pharmacies.

Wedding in 1950 at the Cathedral, Killarney, St John's in Tralee then undergoing renovation.

SELECT PEDIGREE OF THE LATER DENNYS

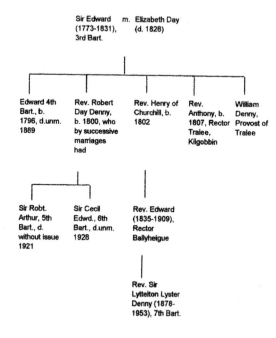

[182] Hussey, *Reminiscences of an Irish Land Agent*, p. 99.

[183] William Feingold, "The Tralee Poor-Law Elections of 1881", in Samuel Clark and James S. Donnelly Jr., *Irish Peasants, Violence and Political Unrest 1780-1914*, Manchester 1983, pp. 285-310; 295-6.

[184] *I.T.*, 8 April 1882.

[185] *I.T.*, 13 Januray 1883.

[186] *I.T.*, 7, 14, 20 October 1882.

[187] *London Times*, 11 January 1883; *I.T.*, 19 January 1883.

[188] M.A. Hickson to William Hartpole Lecky, T.C.D. MS 1827-36, 472, October 10, 1887.

[189] Patrick Foley, *History of the County Kerry, Corkaguiny*, Dublin 1907, pp. 260-261; pp. 265-266; After the 1885 election Harrington became part of an inner group in the Irish Parliamentary Party known as the Bantry Band, which comprised natives of the Beare Peninsula. The very prominent T.M. Healy was a member.

[190] Hickson to Lecky, T.C.D. MS 1827-36, 472, October 10, 1887.

[191] *I.T.*, 7 January 1888.

[192] Bill Power, *White Knights, Dark Earls, The Rise and Fall of an Anglo-Irish Dynasty*, Cork 2000; Michael Lynch, "Edward Harrington and Press Freedom", in *The Kerry Magazine* 2008, p.9.

[193] R. McMorran, "A History of Ballyseedy Wood", in *The Old Kerry Journal*, 2008, p.49.

[194] I am indebetd to Sir Anthony Denny, 8th Bart., for showing me the notes from the diary of his father, Rev. Sir H.L.L. Denny, 7th Bart., on which this paragraph is based.

[195] English National Archives: H.M.C.1/60. It should be added that Mary Hickson's correspondence contains criticism of John J. Gilbert's record as an Inspector of manuscripts in the employ of the H.M.C.; she considered Gilbert's work to have been adversely affected by his nationalism.

[196] Bishop Graves's grandfather was Dean of Ardfert and lived at Sackville during the 1780s. James Graves, prime mover in the Kilkenny Archaeological Society, was a cousin of Bishop Graves.

[197] *K.E.P.*, 27 November 1895.

[198] *Old Kerry Records* appeared decades before the Calendars of State Papers relating to Ireland, Rev. Grosart's Lismore Papers, or that important Kerry source Mrs. Morgan John O'Connell's *The Last Colonel of the Irish Brigade*.

[199] Seán Ó Lúing, *I Die in a Good Cause, Thomas Ashe, Idealist Revolutionary*, Tralee 1970.

[200] "The greatest loss of the 1916 Commandants was Thomas Ashe, because after that time he was the only one with the brains and the standing to lead the nation. There would not have been a Civil War had he lived." This was the opinion of Ned Horan, of Firies, given to George Rice.

[201] T. Ryle Dwyer, *Tans, Terror and Troubles, Kerry's Real Fighting Story 1913-23* (2001), p. 224; Dwyer, *Irish Examiner*, 21 June 2008.

GLOSSARY OF TERMS

Advowson: The right of presentation to a parish.

Undertaker: The term is applied to the leading settlers of the Munster Plantation, those given a tract of land, known as a seignory, and charged with populating it with farmers and tradesmen, and out of which they paid a remittance to the government.

Undertaker is also applied to the leading parliamentary managers, often in opposition, in the Irish House of Commons.

Burgess: The term is interchangeable with Freeman, but with the passage of time, when the freemen elected their representatives to the Corporation, these were known as the burgesses

Recusant: one who refused to conform to the State (Anglican) Church.

Confederate Wars: those wars of the 1640s. *Old Irish* and *Old English* (Anglo-Norman) families, and even some of the *New English*, united under the banner of their shared Catholicism.

Jacobite: the cause of the Scottish dynasty of James II and his successor, the *Old* and *Young Pretender*. James II was overthrown by William of Orange in the Glorious Revolution of 1688,

Penal Laws: legislation to exclude Catholics from state offices, membership of Parliament and corporations such as Tralee, to prohibit the practice of the Catholic religion and ownership of property.

Cess: tax collected by the County Grand Jury.

Appendix I

The Tralee Elections from Incorporation to the Abolition of the Constituency

James I/Charles I/Charles II

1613 Robertus Blenerhassett, Armiger, Humphridus Dethicke, Armiger

1634 Robert Blennerhassett, Sir Beverley Newcomen

1639 Thomas Maule, Armiger, Henricus Osborne, Armiger

1654 Sir Hardress Waller, Sir Henry Ingoldsby

(These gentlemen were called to Cromwell's convention as representatives for Kerry, Limerick and Clare)

1661 John Bennerhassett junior, Armiger, Francis Lynn, Armiger

The Jacobite Parliament

1689 Maurice Hussey, of Kerryie, John Browne, of Ardagh

William and Queen Mary

1692 John Blennerhassett de Ballysheddy, Armiger, Jacobus Waller, Armiger

1695 John St Leger de Doneraile, Frederick Mullins senior, Barry Denny (nephew of Sir Edward Denny) *loco* Johannis St Leger *defuncti*

Queen Anne

1703 Samuel Morris and Arthur Hide, sessions to and including 1711; session 1713 Samuel Morris and Johannes Blennerhassett

George I

1715 Samuel Morris senior, Robert Taylor (1723 Conway Blennerhassett for Samuel Morris, deceased; 1723 William Sprigge for Robert Taylor, deceased; 1725 Luke Gardiner for Conway Blennerhassett, deceased)

George II

1727 John Blennerhassett, Arthur Blennerhassett, ditto all sessions to and including 1741

1743 John Blennerhassett, Thomas Southwell (Dec. 1743 Southwell unseated on petition by Arthur Blennerhassett the younger); sessions 1751, 1753, 1755, 1757, 1759 John Blennerhassett and Arthur Blennhassett

George III

1761 Rowland Bateman, Edward Herbert the Younger; ditto sessions 1763, 1765, 1767

1768 Edward Herbert, the Younger, and Edward Denny; 1771 Edward Denny and Richard Underwood (for Herbert, deceased); ditto 1773; 1775 Richard Underwood and Sir Boyle Roche (who replaces Denny in October after Denny committed suicide)

1776 John Crosbie, John Toler (Thomas Loyd junior for Crosbie in 1777, who elected to serve for Ardfert)

1783 William Godfrey and James Carrique Ponsonby.

1790 Crosbie Morgell and Sir Boyle Roche, ditto sessions 1791, 1792, 1793, 1794

1795 William Fletcher (replaces Morgell who has committed suicide), Fletcher "having since his election accepted the office of one of his Majesty's counsel learned in the law" (king's counsel 1795) and been re-elected; Arthur Moore 1797

1798 Arthur Moore and Henry Kemmis (for James Crosbie and Sir Maurice FitzGerald, Knight of Kerry, respectively, who were elected for Tralee as well as the County but elected to sit for the County)

Westminster Parliament

1801 Arthur Moore

1802 George Canning

1804 George Canning

1806 Sir Maurice FitzGerald, Ballinruddrey

1807 Samuel Boddington Esq. of Upper Brook Street, London, *vice* Maurice FitzGerald, who elected to serve for County Kerry

1807 Sir Arthur Wellesley, Knight of the Bath; Evan Foulkes Esq. of Southampton St. London *vice* Sir A Wellesley, who elected to serve for Newport, Isle of Wight

1808 James Stephen Esq. of Serjeant's Inn, London, vice Evan Foulkes who accepted the Stewartship of the Manor of East Hendred, County Berkshire

1812 Hen Arthur Herbert Esq. of Muckruss, 27 Oct

1813 James Evan Baillie Esq. of the Albany Chambers, Westminster, vice Henry Arthur Herbert Esq.

1818 Edward Denny (son of Sir Edward elected 1828, below)

1819 James Cuff Esq of Deel Castle, County Mayo, *vice* Edward Denny

1820 James Cuff

1826 James Cuff

1828 Sir Edward Denny

1829 Robert Vernon Smith of Savile Row, County Middlesex

1830 Robert Vernon Smith (Aug 18); Dec 4 By-election Smith again returned; no poll

1831 Walker Ferrand, of Harlen Grange, County York

APPENDIX I

1832 Maurice O'Connell (son of The Liberator), 91, (Sir Edward Denny 71)

1835 Maurice O' Connell (85), (William Denny 81)

1837 Aug 7 John Bateman (75), (Maurice O'Connell, L.R. 64). On petition Bateman unseated and O'Connell declared elected on 12 March 1838. Poll amended: O'Connell 133, Bateman 111

1841 Maurice O' Connell, Repeal, 250 (no other).

1847 Maurice O'Connell, R.

1852 Maurice O'Connell

1853 Daniel O'Connell junior (Liberal), replacement for his brother, Maurice

1857 Daniel O'Connell

1859 Daniel O'Connell

1863 O'Connell resigns, is succeeded by Rt. Hon. Thomas O'Hagan (L.)

1865 The O'Donoghue (Daniel O'Donoghue, of the Glens, L.), O'Hagan having accepted appointment as judge of the common pleas

1868 The O'Donoghue

1874 The O'Donoghue

1880 The O'Donoghue (now Home Rule)

Tralee Parish Church (on modern Ashe Street), *Memorials of the Dead*, vol. 7, 1908, the Rev. H. L. L. Denny, author

A list of the year 1291 mentions the "Ecclesia de Tragly". This old church, having been destroyed in the Elizabethan wars, when the last Earl of Desmond was attainted, a new one was erected on or beside its site in (it is said) the year 1587, when the Dennys succeeded the Desmonds as owners of Tralee. This was again destroyed in the rebellion of 1641, rebuilt about ten years later, and demolished once more in 1691 by the Jacobite troops. The present church, or rather its nucleus, was probably erected in or about the year 1700. In the middle of the eighteenth century, when Smith wrote his History of Kerry, it was "a small, plain, oblong building." Within living memory it had galleries all round; and in the chancel (now the north transept) four square pews, two on the ground floor – Denny and Bateman – and two – Blennerhassett and Chute – in the galleries, with fire-places, and curtained all around. These old pews were taken away about 1840; and at this time the coloured windows of the old chancel (now the north transept) were placed there by the Denny family. Subsequently there were erected five coloured windows along the south wall: 1 Crosbie, of Ardfert, with arms and inscription (this was taken down when the present organ was erected); 2 Blennerhassett, with arms and inscription; 3 Spring, with arms and inscription; 4 Denny, with arms and inscription – "Presented by Anthony Denny, rector, and his brothers Henry and William, 1855"; 5 Rowan, with arms and inscription (since taken down). There were afterwards two large stained-glass windows put up at the back of the present galleries, with the arms of Marshal and Hurly. These were destroyed by a storm, and now only the Hurly arms remain.

Kerry Evening Post, 13 November 1895. Annie Rowan.
In Tralee the Friary existed beside the Governor's Castle. It appears to have been connived at until the unrest which culminated in the outbreak of 1641 forced the Governor to forbid the friars to exercise their religion. This obliged the Prior to administer the rites of his Church in secret places.
We may suppose that there was no place of worship for the Roman Catholics in Tralee after the final destruction of White Friars (the Dominicans) until a small chapel was erected at the south of Strand Street, close to Friar's Lane, some time in the middle of the eighteenth century. At the beginning of this present century (the nineteenth, ed.) that chapel was turned into the Tralee theatre, and its remains still existed in 1840. In the forties it was a very unpretending building, almost hidden from Castle Street by two rows of thatched cabins on either side of the

Appendix 2

and leading up to it, which lane is now transformed into a handsome approach. … It was then a very shabby place. After 1850 this chapel began, so to speak, to grow up and show signs of improvement, but the more striking alterations were not attempted until after 1870, when Tralee chapel gradually blossomed into the very handsome edifice which is now an ornament to the town and a credit to its congregation. Arthur Crosbie, builder, carried out this "re-edifying" of St. John's.

In 1839 it (St John's Church of Ireland, Ashe Street) was a very different edifice from what it is today. It then had a gallery all round, great square pews, my father's being a prominent one at the north-west corner, directly opposite the pulpit. The old Communion table stood in the correct canonical position, at the east end of the church. On either side of it were the Denny and Blennerhassett pews. Square rooms, with fireplaces and red curtains on brass rods to shut them off, if desired, from the vulgar view. Upstairs, in the gallery overhead, were two similar pews, fire-places and curtains, occupied respectively by Treasurer Thompson and the Chutes of Chute Hall.

BIBLIOGRAPHY

Ainsworth, John, *The Inchiquin Manuscripts*, Ir. Mss. Comm. 1961,

Berresford Ellis, Peter, *Erin's Blood Royal, The Gaelic Noble Dynasties of Ireland*, 2002,

Bradshaw, Brendan, *The Dissolution of the Religious Orders in Ireland under Henry VIII* (Cambridge 1974),

Burke, Canon William, *The Irish Priests in the Penal Times (1660-1760)*, edn. Patrick Corish, 1968,

Cadet Papers, British Library,

Canning papers, West Yorkshire Archives,

Clarke, Aidan, *The Old English in Irland, 1625-42*, 2000,

Comerford, R.V., *Charles J. Kickham*, 1979,

Comerford, R.V., *The Fenians in Context, Irish Politics and Society 1848-82*, 1985,

Complete Peerage, The,

Conlan, Patrick, OFM, *Franciscan Ireland*, 1978,

Cusack, Mary F., *The History of the Kingdom of Kerry*, 1871,

Denny, Rev. Henry Lyttelton Lyster, *Memorials of the Dead*, vol. 7, 1908, Tralee Parish Church,

Denny, Rev. Sir Henry Lyttelton Lyster, *A Handbook of Co. Kerry Family History*, 1923,

Denny, Rev. Sir Henry Lyttelton Lyster (and others), *The County Kerry Society Annual Reports 1922-40*,

Downey, Declan, "Irish-European Integration, The Legacy of Charles V", in Judith Devlin and Howard B. Clarke (eds.) *European Encounters, Essays in Memory of Albert Lovett* (Dublin 2002), pp. 97-117,

Dwyer, Ryle, *Irish Examiner*, 21 June 2008,

Dwyer, Ryle, Tans, Terror and Troubles, Kerry's Real Fighting Story 1913-23 (2001),

Dunlop, Robert, "The Commonwealth Records", *Archivium Hibernicum*, 1918-21,

Hogan, Edmund, S.J., *The Description of Ireland and The State thereof as it is at this present In Anno 1598*, 1878,

Edwards, David, *The Ormond Lordship in County Kilkenny 1515-1642, The Rise and Fall of Butler, Feudal Power,* Dublin 2003,

Feingold, William, "The Tralee Poor-Law Elections of 1881", in Samuel Clark and James S. Donnelly Jr., *Irish Peasants, Violence and Political Unrest 1780-1914*, Manchester 1983,

Fenton, Seamus, *Kerry Tradition, The Peerless Poets of the Kingdom*, c. 1940,

Fitzmaurice, Lord Edmond, *The Life of William, Earl of Shelburne*, 3 vols. 1875-8,

Flynn, Thomas S., OP, *The Irish Dominicans 1536-1641*, 1993,

Foley, Patrick, *History of the County Kerry, Corkaguiny*, 1907,

BIBLIOGRAPHY

Foster, Joseph, *The Royal Lineage of Our Noble and Gentle Families together with their Paternal Ancestors,* vol. 2, 1887,

Fuller, James Franklin, *Omniana, The Autobiography of an Irish Octogenarian*, 1916,

Fuller, James F. (ed.), "Trial of Rowan Cashel, Attorney, for Murder of Henry Arthur O'Connor, Tralee, 1816", in *Journal of the Cork Historical and Archaeological Society*, vols. 7 and 10, 1901 and 1904,

Gilbert, John J., *History of the Viceroys of Ireland*, Dublin 1865,

Gilbert, John J., *History of the Irish Confederation and the War in Ireland, 1641*-164, 1880-91,

Grosart, Rev. Alexander B., D.D., L.C.D. FSA. (Scot), *The Lismore Papers: Selections from the Private or Public (or State) Correspondence of Sir Richard Boyle never before printed.* 5 vols.,

Hewitt, Esther, *Lord Shannon's Letters to his Son*, Public Record Office Northern Ireland, 1982,

Hickson, Mary, *Old Kerry Records*, series one 1872, series two 1874,

Hoppen, Theodore, *Elections, Politics and Society in Ireland 1833-1855*,

Howard, John, *An Account of the Principal Lazarottos in Europe ...*(Warrington 1789)

Hussey, Rev. Dr Thomas, *A Pastoral Letter to the Catholic Clergy of the United Diocese of Waterford and Lismore*,

Hussey, Samuel, *Reminiscences of an Irish Land Agent*, London 1904,

Hutchinson, Robert, *The Last Days of Henry VIII*, 2005,

Johnston-Liik, Edith, *History of the Irish Parliament 1692-1800*, 2002,

Kelly, Liam, Lucid, Geraldine, O'Sullivan, Maria, *Blennerville, Gateway to Tralee's Past*, 1989,

Kerry's Fighting Story 1916-1921, Told by the Men Who Made It,

Kinealy, Christine, *The Great Calamity, The Irish Famine 1845-52*, 1994,

King, Jeremiah, *History of Kerry, or History of the Parishes in the County,* 1908-14,

King, William, *The State of the Protestants of Ireland Under the Late King James's Government*, London 1691,

Lecky Mss, TCD,

Lehane, Shane, *The Great Famine in the Poor Law Unions of Dingle and Killarney, Co. Kerry, 1845-52*, (M.A. thesis National University of Ireland, U.C.C. 2005),

Lewis, Samuel, *A Topographical Dictionary of Ireland*, London 1837,

Lucey, Donnacha Sean, *The Irish National League in Dingle, County Kerry, 1885-1892*, 2003,

Lyne, Gerald J., *The Lansdowne Estate in Kerry under W.S. Trench 1849-72*, Dublin 2001,

MacCarthy Murrogh, Michael, *The Munster Plantation, English Migration to Southern Ireland 1583-1641*, 1986,

Magennis, Eoin, *The Irish Political System 1740-1765, The Golden Age of the Undertakers*, Dublin 2000,

Maxwell, Constantia, *Dublin Under The Georges*, 1936,

McConville, Seamus (ed.), *The Dominicans of Tralee*, 1987,

McCormack, Anthony M., *The Earldom of Desmond 1463-1583, the Decline and Crisis of a Feudal Lordship*, 2005,

McMorran, Russell, and O'Keeffe, Maurice, *A Pictorial History of Tralee*, 2005,

Munter, Robert, *A Dictionary of the Print trade in Ireland 1550 -1775*, New York 1988,

Norris, John, *Shelburne and Reform*, 1963,

Ó Corrbuí, Mairtin, *Kenry, The Story of a Barony in County Limerick*, 1975,

Ó Lúing, Seán, *I Die in a Good Cause, Thomas Ashe, Idealist Revolutionary*, Tralee 1970,

O'Connell, Mrs. Morgan John, *The Last Colonel of the Irish Brigade*, 1892,

O'Daly, Dominic, *The Rise, Increase and Exit of the Geraldines, Earls of Desmond*, translated C.P. Meehan, Dublin 1878,

Ó Riordain, John J., *Where Araglen So Gently Flows*, 2007,

O'Sullivan, Donal J., *The Church of St John the Evangelist, Ashe Street, Tralee*, 2001,

O'Sullivan, Thomas F., *Romantic Hidden Kerry*, Tralee 1931,

Power, Bill , *White Knights, Dark Earls, The Rise and Fall of an Anglo-Irish Dynasty*, Cork 2000,

Rowan, Archdeacon Arthur Blennerhassett, *Tralee and its Provost Sixty Years On, with introduction by The Last of its Provosts*, 24 copies printed, 1860,

Rowan, Rev. Archdeacon Arthur Blennerhassett, *A Plea from the Protestants of Ireland, to the Right Hon. Lord Morpeth, Chief Secretary for Ireland*, Dublin 1840,

Rowe, Eddie, Tralee Court House, *Kerry's Eye*, 29 April, 27 May, 16, 30 June, 15, 22 July 1978,

Russell, Thomas, *Relation of the FitzGeralds of Ireland, written in the County of Clare 22 Oct, 1638* (*Journal of the Historical and Archaeological Association of Ireland*, 1868-9),

Sayles, G.O., "The Rebellious First Earl of Desmond", in Watt, Morrall and Mant, *Medieval Studies Presented to Aubrey Gwynn, S.J.*, Dublin 1961, pp. 203-229,

Smith, Charles, *The Antient and Present State of the County and City of Cork*, 2 vols. 1750,

Smith, Charles, *The Antient and Present State of The County of Kerry* 1756,

Smith, W. J., *Herbert Correspondence*, University of Wales, 1963,

St. John D. Seymour, B. D., *Adventures and Experiences of a XVIIth Century Clergyman, edited from the Original Manuscript*, Dublin 1909,

Storey, G., *A True and Impartial History of the Kingdom of Ireland During the Two last Years*, London 1691,

Thornley, David, *Isaac Butt and Home Rule*, 1964,

BIBLIOGRAPHY

Townshend, Dorothea Baker, *The Life and Letters of the Great Earl of Cork*, London 1904,

Treadwell, Victor, *The Irish Commission of 1622* (Irish Mss. Commission 2006),

Wall, Maureen, *Catholic Ireland in the Eighteenth Century, Collected Essays*, edited by Gerard O'Brien and Tom Dunne, 1989,

Walsh, T.J., *Nano Nagle and the Presentation Sisters*, Dublin 1959,

Wellington Papers, WP1/1239/10, Hartley Library, University of Southampton,

Wright, Edward, Mathematician, "The Voyage of the Earl of Cumberland to the Azores in 1589", in *Arber's English Garner: Voyages and Travels*, vol. II, 1903.

Acts, Reports, Calendars, Commissions

Act. 5 Geo. 3, c. 20, An Act for erecting and establishing public infirmaries; 7 Geo 3, c. 8,

Act. 46 George 3, cap. 142, An Act for vesting the settled Estates of Sir Edward Denny ...,

Local Government and Taxation of Towns Inquiry Commission (Ireland, including Tralee), 1877,

A List of Officers in the Several Regiments and Independent Troops and Companies of Militia in Ireland, taken from the Books in the Secretaries' Offices, Dublin. Printed in the year 1761,

British Parliamentary Papers, vol. xxvii, Local Government in Southern Ireland 1835, *Reports from the Commissioners on the Municipal Corporations in Ireland 1835, Borough of Tralee,*

Calendars: *State Papers. Carew 1575-88; 1603-24; Cal. Documents, Ireland, 1285-1292, 1293-1301; Cal. State Papers 1574-1585; Cal. State Papers Ireland, James I, 1606-1608; State Papers, Ireland, Reign of Elizabeth January 1598-March 1599; Cal.Patent and Close Rolls of Chancery Ireland 18th to the 45th of Queen Elizabeth*, vol. 2 (ed. Morrin),

Endowed Schools Commission, 2 vols, 1857 (Tralee evidence of 1855),

Evidence taken before the commissioners appointed to enquire into the occupation of land in Ireland (the *Devon Commission*, 1844),

The Irish Fiants of The Tudor Sovereigns, vol. 3 *Queen Elizabeth I*, 1994,

Report of the Select Committee of the House of Lords 1825, Disturbances in Ireland,

Report on the state of Hospitals, Infirmaries and Public Dispensaries, Journal of the Irish House of Commons, vol. 12 (1788),

Reports from the Commissioners on the Municipal Corporations in Ireland 1835, Borough of Tralee,

Journal of the Kerry Archaeological and Historical Society

FitzSimons, Robert, *Medicine and Society in Nineteenth-Century Kerry*, 1994,

MacCotter, Paul, *Lordship and Colony in Anglo-Norman Kerry*, 2004,

MacCurtain, Sister Margaret, *The Fall of the House of Desmond*, 1975,

BIBLIOGRAPHY

MacSweeney, Marie, *Blennerville 1088-1853 – the Shifting Fortunes of a Kerry Village*, 2003,

McCarthy, Brendan G., *The Surrender of an Armada Vessel near Tralee; an Exploration of the State Papers*, 1990,

Nicholls, K.W., *The FitzMaurices of Kerry*, 1970, p. 40-41,

O'Shea, Fr Kieran, *David Moriarty (1814-77)*, 1970, 1971, 1972, 1973,

O'Shea, Rev. Kieran, *Bishop Moylan's Relatio Status*, 1785, 1974. pp 21-36,

S.M., *Some Old Tralee Notes*, 1997.

Articles from *The Kerry Magazine*, with year of publication

Bary, Valerie, *The Square at Milltown*, 2001,

Chambers, Liam, *The Irish Colleges in 17th- and 18th- Century Paris: A Brief History*, 2009,

Curtin, Danny, *Edward Harrington and the First GAA Event in Kerry*, 2000,

Lynch, Michael, *Edward Harrington and Press Freedom*, 2008,

MacMahon, Bryan, *Sir Redvers Buller in Kerry*, 2003,

McMorran, Russell, *The Tralee Elections of 1852*, 2001,

McMorran, Russell, *Archdeacon Rowan, Founder of The Kerry Magazine*, 1989,

Ó Concubhair, Padraig, *Comoradh '98: How Kerry celebrated the Centenary of a Revolution*, 1999,

Ó Concubhair, Padraig, *The Society of St Vincent de Paul in Dingle – 1846*, 2000,

O'Carroll, Gerald, *Middle-Georgian Elections in Kerry: Contending Commitments to Accountability and Graft*, 2002,

O'Sullivan, Donal, *Laying the Atlantic Cable*, 2000,

O'Toole, Joe, *Corcha Dhuibhne in 1916 and the First Kerry President of the Irish Republic*, 2007.

Other Journals and Newspapers

Berland, Kevin, " 'Chesterfield Demands the Muse': Anglo-Irish Poets Publishing the 'Irish' Voice, 1745-6" in *Eighteenth-Century Ireland, Iris an dá chultúr*, vol. 17, 2002,

Denny, *Notes and Queries*, 8 September 1923 (transcription of original letter to the Queen from the Tralee settlers is in the possession of Sir Anthony Denny),

Bradley, John, "The Medieval Towns of Kerry", in *North Munster Antiquarian Journal*, 1986,

Bric, Maurice J. "The Tithe System in Eighteenth-Century Ireland", in *Proceedings of the Royal Irish Academy*, vol. 86, 1986,

Caball, John, "The Siege of Tralee, 1642", in *The Irish Sword* 1954-56,

BIBLIOGRAPHY

Denny, Rev. Sir H.L.L., "Biography of Sir Edward Denny, Knight Banneret, of Bishop's Stortford, Herts., Gentleman of the Privy chamber to Queen Elizabeth, Governor of Kerry and Desmond", *Transactions of the East Herts Archaeological Society*, vol. 2 part 3, (originally prepared for the *Hertfordshire Dictionary of Biography*), appeared subsequently in the *Kerry Evening Post* of 22 and 26 September 1906,

Dunlop, Robert, "An Unpublished Survey of the Plantation of Munster in 1622" in *Journal of the Royal Society of Antiquaries of Ireland*, vol. 54, 1924,

Graves, Rev. James, "The Earls of Desmond, Unpublished Geraldine Documents", in *Journal of the Royal Society of Antiquaries of Ireland*, 1869,

Hayman, Canon, "The Geraldines of Desmond", in *Journal of the Archaelolgical Association of Ireland*, 1881,

Hickson, Mary, "The Knights of St John in Kerry and Limerick", in *Journal of the Royal Historical and Archaeological Association in Ireland*, vol. 9, 1889,

MacCarthy (Glas), Daniel, Appendix to "Unpublished Geraldine Documents", in *J.A.A.I.* 1869,

MacCurtain, Margaret, "An Irish Agent of the Counter-Reformation, Dominic O'Daly", in *Irish Historical Studies*, September 1967,

McElligott, Maurice G., "Some Kerry Wild Geese", in *The Irish Genealogist*, vol. 2, no. 8, October 1950,

McMorran, Russell, "A History of Ballyseedy Wood", in *The Old Kerry Journal*, 2008,

Ó Corráin, Donncha, "Some Historical References to Killorglin", in *Cois Leamhna, Journal of Killorglin History and Folklore Society*, Killarney 1984,

O'Cleary's, Michael, *The Book of Pedigrees*, in Canon Hayman, "The Geraldines of Desmond", in *Journal of the Archaeolgical Association of Ireland*, 1879-82,

Sloane Ms. no. 10081 (anon.), in Herbert Webb Gillman, "The Rise and Progress in Munster of the Rebellion, 1642", *Journal of the Cork Historical and Archaeological Society*, November 1895,

Rowan, Archdeacon Arthur B., *The Kerry Magazine*

Westropp, Thomas Johnson, "The Desmond Castle Newcastle West, Co. Limerick", in *J.R.S.A.I*, 1909/1910, reprint 1983

Munster News and Provincial Advertiser,

Tralee Chronicle ,

Hibernian Chronicle, William *Flin's* (Cork),

Western Herald,

INDEX

INDEX

INDEX

INDEX

Index

INDEX

INDEX

INDEX

INDEX

INDEX

INDEX

Ogham stones, 125

Old Kerry Records, 33, 125, 134

Orde, Thomas, Chief Secretary, 71

Ormond, 4th Earl, 12

Ormond, family, 10

Ormond, James, 12th Earl, Duke, 44, 47, 49

Ormond, territory, 21, 29 (caption), 40

Ormond, Tom, 10th Earl, 21, 23-25, 28, 29

Orrery (Brighill), Roger Boyle, Earl, 42, 44, 47, 48-9, 59

Ossory (bishop), 66

Oxford (Movement), 104

Oxford, 78

Palatinate (Desmond), 9

Palatinate (German), 64

Palatine community, 64, 73

Pale, the, 48

Palmerston, Viscount (Henry Temple, Lord), 108

Paris, Le Journal de, 128

Parnell, Charles Stewart, 113, 118-19, 124

Pastorini, 96

Pavia, 18

Peel, Sir Robert, PM, 89, 99, 103-104, 106

Pelham, Ld. Deputy, 23

Pembroke, Countess of, 27

Pembroke, Earl of, 27

Penal Laws, 56, 71

Penn, William, 71

Pennefather, Baron,

Pennsylvania, 71

Perceval, Spenser, 86, 88

Petty, Anne, 56, see Lady Kerry,

Petty, Charles, 50

Philip II, 21

Philip III, 37

Philip the Bold, 10

Phoenix Park (murders), 119-20

Phoenix Society, 108

Pierrepoint, Albert, 130

Pigot's Directory 1824, 103

Pikeman, Tralee, 125

Pitt, William, PM, 67, 70-1, 85

Pius IX, Pope, (Pio Nono), 108

Plan of Campaign, 120-22, 127

Playboy of the Western World, 124

Plymley Letters, 98

Pococke, Richard (Bishop), 66

Poff, Sylvester, 119-120

Poor Law Amendment Act 1847,

Poor Law unions, 105

Porter, 52

Portland, Duke of, 78

Portrinard, Castle, 10

Portsmouth, 51

Portugal, 10, 46, 83

Poynings' Law, 73

Presentation Sisters, 87

Pretender (Old), 58

Pretender, (Bonnie P. Charlie, Young P.), 62-3

Protestant Reformation, 19

Prussia, 70

Puritans, 37, 40

Puseyism, 104

Quarter Acre (Gregory) Clause, 105

Queen's Colleges, 104, 111

Raleigh, Sir Walter, 24, 26, 27, 28, 31

Rathass, 6, 102

Rathfarnham, 57

Rathkeale, 60, 64

Rathmines, 130

Rathmore, 96

Rattass, 6

Rattoo, 6

Raymond,

Rebel Earl, see Gerald

Rebellion (1798), 80, 82, 125

Rebellion (Easter 1916), 125-7

Red Shard, 42

Redmond, John, 124

Regency Crisis, 77

Regent, Prince (William IV), 88

Repeal,

Restoration (land) settlement, 46

INDEX

INDEX

INDEX

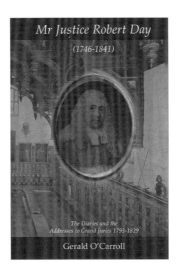

Hardback, 337 pages, 45 euros. Polymath Press 2004,
Polymaths Booksellers, Courthouse Lane, Tralee

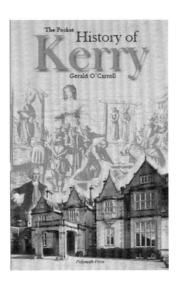

The Pocket History of Kerry, by Gerald O'Carroll, price 25 euros, hardback, 2007,
ISBN 978-0-9547902-1-9. Publishers Polymaths Booksellers, Courthouse Lane, Tralee